Running
from the
Devil

Running
from the
Devil

HOW I SURVIVED A STOLEN CHILDHOOD

SARA DAVIES

JOHN BLAKE

Published by John Blake Publishing Ltd,
3 Bramber Court, 2 Bramber Road,
London W14 9PB, England

www.blake.co.uk

First published in paperback in 2007

ISBN: 978 1 84454 413 4

British Library Cataloguing-in-Publication Data:

A catalogue record for this book is available from the British Library.

Design by www.envydesign.co.uk

Printed in the UK by CPI Bookmarque, Croydon, CR0 4TD

3 5 7 9 10 8 6 4 2

Papers used by John Blake Publishing are natural, recyclable products made from
wood grown in sustainable forests. The manufacturing processes conform to the
environmental regulations of the country of origin.

Every attempt has been made to contact the relevant copyright-holders,
but some were unobtainable. We would be grateful if the appropriate
people could contact us.

Acknowledgements

There are many people that supported me through my writing. Therefore, I'm not sure where to start, I just hope that I don't miss anyone out; if I do, then you all know that I really do appreciate your support. First of all, I'd like to thank Linda, my closest friend, with all my heart. You supported me through a very tough time and I'm sure that your head must still be banging. Bruno, thank you for the lengthy telephone conversations. They cost us both a fortune, but they were worth it, you are a true gem and a real clever clogs.

I'd also like to show my appreciation to Denise Robertson, the effort that you put in to helping so many men, women and children is amazing. I truly admire your strength. And I'm so glad that I had yours and all of your friends' support on Dear Denise during those dark moments when I felt like giving up. Thank you.

To Michelle Signore. Thank you for seeing past the odd few spelling mistakes and having enough faith in my story to put it to print, for all of your hard work and patience and for helping me to fulfil my promise to Nana. To John

Blake and all at John Blake Publishing, a really big heartfelt thank you.

To Laura Holman, author of *Behind the Mask*. From the first moment that we talked you got it, you knew exactly what I was feeling; the turmoil that I felt while dredging up all of those terrible memories, some that may not have reared their ugly heads for years to come, but while writing they came thick and fast and sometimes left me breathless. Thank you for being a breath of fresh air, and such an understanding fellow survivor. You are one tough cookie. A true inspiration.

Many thanks to Sue William Silverman, author of *Because I Remember Terror, Father, I Remember You* and *Love Sick*. You are the first person that I spoke with about my writing and you told me the only way to do this was to write from the heart, and that it didn't matter about my lack of schooling because I had a real story to tell that could possibly help many others. I truly appreciate those words because they gave me the strength and determination to keep writing. Thank you!

To Mum and Dad, I wouldn't be the strong-willed person that I am today if it wasn't for both of you. I now know how to be a real mother and, something which neither of you can do, I can walk with my head held high and have strength that even both of you put together could never have.

To protect identities, all names have been changed in this book.

Contents

Introduction

We sometimes feel like a tiny speck when we consider how huge the universe is. In truth, we all have a part to play in keeping the world going and making sure that we leave something behind for future generations to learn from. Keeping that in mind has helped me to keep my life in perspective. I'm now left, at the age of thirty, with a wider view, and able to look at the whole picture, not just concentrate on the huge things in life. I can also look at the tiny details and figure out why, and how, I got where I am today.

Until I started writing this book, I went through life feeling victimised, holed up, bullied and angry with the world, to the point where I hid myself away and often felt trapped, scared and very much alone. But I convinced myself that to be cautious is very wise and that I was doing the right thing by protecting myself from any more harm. Now that I've faced my demons, I can see that while I was hiding myself away I was missing ample opportunities for nourishment and growth.

Because of the abuse in my early years, I was bullied out of what I deserved – a normal life, with love, comfort and safety and a family I could confide in. I gave those out there that have abused me more power than they deserve, and now it's my turn to live, succeed, socialise and speak out without fear of being shot down.

I came to the conclusion that, although my past couldn't change, I could definitely change my future by putting a stop to the way I kept on reliving my past. Every day my father would constantly be on my mind, and lots of little reminders were there, simple things like walking past a father and daughter and feeling jealous because I'd never be able to do that. I felt cheated, hurt and desperate for some answers, which is another reason for my putting pen to paper and writing this book.

I can't say that I've found myself again, because I'll never know who I should have been. I was a child for many years, a child with many personalities, a child that wasn't sure of herself, because she didn't have room to grow, a child that most of the time was lost in a dreamlike state to distract herself from the pain and suffering she was enduring. No, I'll never know who I should have been, but I like the new me, and it feels good to be living for the first time in my life. At last I've been born and, although it may be a little late in the day, I'm ready to take my life and turn it around to the full.

I have not written this book to try to pull on anyone's heartstrings and gain sympathy, nor do I want to come across as though I have a holier-than-though attitude and I know it all, because, quite frankly, I don't. I don't have all the answers. I couldn't begin to tell the individual how to move on from any painful experience that they've endured as a child. I have simply written this for me and, hopefully, to show all those who have suffered, or are suffering, physical, mental or sexual abuse that all is not lost. That it is possible to find the strength and resolve to break out from the cycle of abuse and make a new life. It is not easy — it takes courage, determination, self-belief and good timing, especially as life after abuse is full of uncertainties.

The decision to write about my life was a very difficult one because this is a true story. While some of the events described here may seem like a fictional horror tale, they are fact. And they are not as rare as the authorities would have you believe. Names and places have been changed because this account tells of vulnerable people on whom further suffering must not be inflicted.

I hope that my story will help many to see that, after

such a terrible invasion of one's childhood, trusting one's fellow humans is very, very hard. Most abusers are very convincing liars, so getting to the point where you, the abused, are actually believed is a very big step, and one that can be extremely difficult to take.

The message I am trying to get across to all sufferers of mental, physical and all other forms of abuse, whether as a child or as an adult, is: be strong, be resolute and freedom shall be yours!

1

My Father

I dare not, I cannot sleep. He may enter my room. What if he's drunk? Surely he will be. He always is, and the pungent smell of alcohol is in the air whenever he's around. I hope he doesn't hurt me too much.

Those are thoughts that ran through my mind again and again from a very young age. I had many sleepless nights, never knowing if I'd be safe in my own bed. Terrified of the one man that I should have been able to feel safe with. My father.

I was raised on a characterless estate — not a very nice place to live, but we got by. My father was the local drug dealer, my mother worked in a local factory. Father was a well-respected member of the community, with a number of friends from different racial backgrounds and lifestyles. My mother and father held all-night blues parties most weekends. I'd often help out behind the breakfast bar. We'd serve up spicy, salty food cooked by my mum. She believed that by giving them enough to make their throats burn they'd keep on coming back to me for the booze. Father's friends weren't fazed at all by the fact that a child was selling them alcohol, but they would occasionally call me over and give me the odd fiver. I suppose, when I think about it now, it was their conscience biting back at them.

My parents must have made a packet, what with the blues parties, selling drugs, her job, Dad's dole money and his income from the other women. Instead of using the money to attain their goal, which was to make a better life for themselves, they would buy the other children on the estate. Every day at least two of them were in our home, quite often eating our food and sleeping in our beds, drunk. Father would make us sleep on the floor after palming us off with a bit of porridge, while they got the special treat of a curry and a cosy bed. He looked after them in such a way that it became unbelievable he could be anything other than a good man.

The fathers of those children began to kiss his backside after he started hiding guns around the house and in the back garden for them. They'd go off and do their armed robberies, and afterwards he'd help them cover their tracks, putting his own kids at risk in the process. Until my brother and his friend dug up a handgun in our garden, they were just being typical little boys, digging around for worms. They took it straight into the house to my dad. He quickly brushed it off, saying it was probably a soldier's gun from the war, and assured them that he'd take it to the police station. We all believed him at the time — even my mother seemed convinced — but it's obvious now that he was lying, because the estate was newly built. I'm sure the council workmen would have noticed a gun while they were creating the garden. The estate was full of similar tales, with many people covering up for each other and the biggest rule being 'no grasses'. Going to the police about anyone was the biggest crime you could commit.

There were many single-parent families struggling to get by financially. A lot of them were still living with their parents, some with just the grandmother. Mostly big families, they were crammed into small two- or three-bedroom maisonettes. Young mums had sons who were committing crimes by the age of ten and daughters who were getting pregnant, sometimes as young as 13, and were totally out of control. The girls were simply following in their mothers' footsteps and the result was a high rate of teenage pregnancy. The boys, wanting to be just like their fathers, put themselves at great risk of going to prison, or even of dying in violent and terrible circumstances at an early age.

Most of the young girls getting pregnant were bored as

there was nothing much to do on the estate. A very high percentage of them turned to drugs, with many quickly becoming addicts and ensuring their unborn babies got a terrible start in life. In almost all cases, as soon as a child was born he or she was doomed to failure, never getting the chance to see a different and better way of life.

Almost everyone on the estate had been there all their life. With no opportunity to get out, they didn't know any better — although not many wanted to leave in any case, because they were so used to the lifestyle they had. From what Mum has told me, even back in the second half of the 1970s and the 1980s, the place was so violent that it was a no-go area for the police. Lacking any choice, most residents stayed put and simply fought for survival. Some became desperate and there were many suicide attempts, some of them successful. Suicide became such a regular occurrence that the train line that ran across the back of our home started to feel like a graveyard. Even young children would stand in front of a train out of desperation.

With no real idea of an alternative, people took drugs out of sheer boredom and fought among themselves. Most of them were struggling to feed their children and afford drugs at the same time. This left the kids not only starving but also heading in the same direction as their parents — towards a life of crime and self-destruction. By contrast, my father started making a packet out of the estate's deprived and vulnerable by selling them drugs at a price that was high financially as well as physically and mentally.

To this day, I still hear rumours about how he 'loaned' drugs to tenants, making them think he was doing them a big favour. In fact, he truly believed that he was bringing something to their lives. Apparently, if any of the females couldn't pay him for their drugs at the end of the week, they'd sleep with him instead. From what I hear, getting his leg over every fool that would take him suited him fine. Most of them had his little sprogs running around the estate, and having those kids gave him a different woman he could go to every night of the week.

By the time my mother knew about my father's terrible ways, she was too involved to question his behaviour. His party lifestyle and newfound fortune came to an abrupt end when he became paranoid and convinced himself that the council were bugging us; he decided it was safer to stop the blues parties. He insisted that they were around, and would go into a great panic if he heard so much as a pin drop on the estate late at night. Clearly, the burden of being Mr Big was getting to him.

It felt fantastic that summer to see him on his knees, by moonlight, digging up his marijuana plants from the garden. He put the plants in some big dustbins in my bedroom and bought some heavy-duty net curtains for my window. His paranoia had kicked in and he would stroll across the road to make sure that nobody could see the plants from the other buildings. The way he was acting, if I'd lived across the road I would have been very suspicious of his actions. Somehow, he got away with it. Again, my mother never questioned him as to why he would want to grow drugs in his kid's bedroom. She feared him too much.

I remember once pulling a leaf off one of his precious plants. He caught me and made me eat it. For hours afterwards, I didn't feel very well, but he wouldn't give me as much as a glass of water to take away the bitter taste. It was horrible, it made my head go all fuzzy and I felt terrible for days. I never touched the stuff again. I remember him saying to me, 'Don't touch my shit. I hope it fucking kills you next time.'

Even without bringing in the abuse that I endured from my father, I can see now that both my parents had strange ideas on how to punish their children. From time to time, I'd try to grasp my mother's attention, often wishing that she could see my pain and suffering, but most of the time she seemed quite angry and full of pain herself. She often cried herself to sleep at night, then the following day would scream at us for the simplest little things, like if we hadn't put the sugar back in the exact spot where it should be. Or maybe when it was something that called for a motherly hug, say if one of us had fallen over and was crying, she'd scream, 'Shut up, shut up,' and start foaming at the mouth. Many times, she would threaten us, 'You wait until your dad gets home.' At those words, we'd quake in our boots and behave for the rest of the day. Even though she knew that he would beat us, depending on her mood she might tell him that we'd misbehaved. In fact, often she sat back and watched us get beaten. Then they'd put us to bed early and sit on the sofa snuggling up to each other.

But my mother wasn't always that way. Sometimes she would protect us from Dad's beatings, often lying to him to stop him from hurting us. The other times, I suppose, she'd got fed up with having to spend a fortune on eye shadow to cover up her black eyes and had found a way to distract him from hitting her. Maybe she thought it was easier to watch her kids get a beating instead of taking one herself.

I believe my father learned most of his vicious ways from his parents. Luther and Joyce were very strict, some would say sick. I don't call them Nana and Granddad, as I don't believe they've earned those titles. They have seven children, three girls and four boys. All of them were beaten daily with broomsticks, belts and various other objects. Ray, my father, was the first to leave home, to be with my mum, which really upset them, as they were convinced he'd left to get away from them. In hindsight, they must have realised that their physical abuse of their children was wrong.

They hated my mother. Originally, they were angry that Dad was marrying a white woman. They said that he was West Indian and, just because he'd been in the country for three or four years by the time he met my mum, he didn't need to start acting like a white man. The four of them had a very strange relationship, often arguing among themselves then making up for a couple of years before falling out again. They never really had a good word to say about one another.

One time Joyce called my father to say that my uncle Graham, who lived in the West Indies, was ill. According to her, he'd had a car crash and was in intensive care, so all her kids had to club together to pay for the hospital bills. At first, Dad believed her, but after he'd talked to all his brothers and sisters it became clear that she was lying. He then enticed her to our house by saying that he had a few grand waiting for her. But when she arrived he gave her a mouthful. I remember it so clearly, especially as it was so shocking to hear him talk to his mother like that. 'You fucking money-hungry, fat old bitch' was one insult I recall. Those words infuriated her, and quite rightly so. She ran towards him, but he grabbed her by the hair and threw her out of the house. I thought that would be the end of the matter, but half an hour later she was back.

A cascade of two-pence coins started spilling through the letterbox, then she started ranting, 'You and your kids will never have anything. You gonna suffer for the rest of your lives. Voodoo, voodoo, obia man a go haunt you for the rest of your fucking lives, you dirty mongrels.' I swear those words stick with me to this day, and I have never looked at a two-pence coin in the same way since. They fell out for at least six months over that incident and didn't make up until my uncle Graham miraculously recovered and came to visit us. Joyce then turned up with her tail between her legs. Everyone made up and our happy family was back together again. Well, not quite – my mother still took the blame for anything that went wrong with the family, Joyce always referring to her as 'the white bitch'. Mum accepted everything her in-laws threw at her, and often took us to visit them over the weekend, acting as though we were a normal family.

I feared just about everyone that my father knew, from his mother and father to his best friend. I can't remember ever feeling safe in my home. It was a very confusing time, especially as my mother's parents were so fantastic. They were great and we really looked forward to their visits. Nana came to see us nearly every day, Granddad most weekends. The difference between our two sets of grandparents was remarkable. We had the raving loonies on the one side and the quiet conservatives on the other. It's a good job that we kids had Nana and Granddad to look forward to.

My mother truly believed – in fact, insisted – that my dad's behaviour was the normal action of a black man. She'd often told me that all black men hit their women and kids. It was just an accepted part of being with a black man, she would say. She stressed to me that one thing the woman should never try to do was leave him, or call the police, because he would kill her if he found her. What I never understood is what used to follow that warning. She'd say, 'If you ever go out with a white man I'll disown you. Yuk! No way is a daughter of mine going out with a pig. I have never, and will never, let a white man touch me.'

She used to confuse me with her weird opinions, and even at a young age I used to think, Well, you're white and so are Nana and Granddad, so what is so wrong with white people? I'm half-white. Why does she hate white men so much? But she often repeated those words to me and, being a young and impressionable child, for a while I believed her and started to think the same way. I always believed my mother, as any child would. Besides, I wanted so much to feel like her daughter and not just a Giro that she received every two weeks I was willing to accept all her ramblings.

Not many people can say that their mother is a puppeteer. I'd like to be able to say it's a privilege that mine is, but I can't claim to feel any pride when I say that's what she is. My mother was never one to show affection towards me and my brothers and sisters. She often left us feeling as though we were the adults and she was the child. We took care of the home, arguments, family fun and joyous occasions, while she sat back and lapped it all up. I believe that she resented having us to take care of but needed us to make her feel as though she'd achieved something with her life.

My Father

I'll never understand why my mother went so wrong. She'd had a regular, stable family upbringing with loving parents, so the way she is now seems all the more baffling. At the age of 11, she started rebelling against Nana and Granddad's every wish. Playing outside with her friends until all hours; sneaking out when she had been grounded by Granddad; driving Nana to the point where she once tried to reshape her face by hitting her over the head with a frying pan. Nana still gets embarrassed when she tells me that story, but I suppose that hitting her daughter with anything at all, let alone something so heavy, was due to a mixture of anger and disbelief. Nana has often stressed how she had tried so hard to raise her kids with respect, yet her daughter was treating her as though she'd been a bad mother and neglected her. And repeatedly she has told me that she'd go into Mum's room to check on her during the night and find her bed empty. Sometimes she'd find her at her friend's house across the road, but more often than not she had to sit up and wait until Mum got back home in the early hours of the morning.

Nana and Granddad also disapproved of the fact that she hung around with all the black kids at school. Nana has always denied being racist but, from what she told me, they were worried about their daughter going out with a black man, or what they called back then in the seventies 'a coloured person'. She says that it was common then to feel that way, and assures me that she soon got used to the idea after we were born and loved us all no matter what colour we were.

My mother bought most of her school friends by helping out the more underprivileged of them with a bit of lunch money. It was at school that she became very close friends with my aunt, which is how she met my father. Nowadays, she admits that she got close to Auntie Helen so that she could get to know Dad. She'd had enough of admiring him from a distance. By the time my parents started dating, my dad had already left school but my mum was only in her second year. They managed to keep their relationship a secret from Nana and Granddad for three years, until she had no choice when, at the age of 15, she fell pregnant with my brother Carl. Somehow, her pregnancy was kept secret for quite a while but by the time she was almost five months pregnant there was little way of hiding her bump, so the two of them had to tell Nana.

Granddad left Nana to deal with the entire thing. It's something he has often done – if he was ever disappointed with anyone, he would cut them off for a while as he didn't like to show his anger. I have often wondered if he was scared of what he might do to them; if maybe he was a bit aggressive underneath his nice, kind smile. He liked to be calm and steered clear of losing his temper. I suppose he's what some would call a real gentleman.

The way my mother treated my grandparents has often

made me wonder if she was a spoiled child, or maybe it was a way of getting a little more attention, as she was the youngest of three children. But, knowing my grandparents, I'm sure she was treated exactly the same as her brother and sister. So my inability to understand her behaviour remains to this day. Perhaps I'll never know why my mother is the way she is.

2

Rays of Sunshine

From a very young age, I was what you might call mentally overdeveloped. I knew much more than the other kids in my class did. When most of them would swear and be asked what it meant, they'd shrug their shoulders, but I knew what most swear words meant. 'Fuck' was the first I learned. My father would often say it to me in a childlike voice and giggle, as though he couldn't believe he was getting away with it. He'd then tell me that he could only show me what it meant.

By the age of five, I knew what sex was and what 'cheating' meant, not only because I had seen that kind of behaviour in my home but also because I was being subjected to several hours of what I can only describe as physical and mental torture. Although my father had touched my vagina and often rubbed himself against me from as long ago as I can remember, it wasn't until my fifth birthday that he took the abuse to another level. He'd decided that from that day on I was going to be his lover and not his daughter.

Most weekends I was at my grandparents' and, although this arrangement wasn't always rosy, at least I had a little time away from my father and his monstrous ways. Our grandparents on both sides took it in turn to have my brother Carl and me to stay with them, but we dreaded going to Dad's parents. But, even though they abused us and were absolutely horrifying to be with, staying with them didn't seem half as bad as being at home with our drunken skunk of a father.

These weekends away from home lasted for about two years, until my mother decided that she didn't want to go out to blues parties with my father any more because she couldn't handle the number of women that she was fighting with over him. Whenever they dropped us off at my dad's parents', we were guaranteed a beating from our grandfather. As soon as they walked away from the house, our chests would pound with fear. We knew that it was just a matter of time before he took off his belt and thrashed us, as though we were his Alsatian guard dog, which he kept in the garden and often beat for no apparent reason. He would say that the dog needed teaching a lesson and a dog is just a filthy animal that needs to be kept in its place. So, when he was beating us while calling us 'fucking dirty mongrels', we started to believe that we were just as filthy and deserved as little respect as his dog.

Carl and I became so fearful of our dad's parents that we would start to scream at them to take us to Nana and Granddad's house as soon as my parents walked away. We realised that it was a big mistake to make so much noise early on, when he started sending us to his room straight away. He would tell us to lie face down on the bed and then follow us up the stairs after kissing my mother goodbye and patting my father on the back as he told them that we would be fine. His beatings were very severe. I could tell by the way that he whipped us that he was the person who had trained my father how to use his belt on us. The only thing that was different about the beating from our grandfather was the fact that his belt was ten times thicker than our dad's. He must have gone out and bought a thicker one every year, as though his beating wasn't good enough and he wasn't getting his fix any more.

Our grandmother would stand and watch him, as though she had to make sure he had done a good enough job on us. She would often say, 'Next time you come, if you're better behaved, then you won't get a beating, will you? Luther, when you've finished, send them fucking pickneys downstairs to me, because them have some chores to do.'

We'd then drag our sore, tiny bodies down the stairs

and start our tasks. First of all, we'd have to pick up the dog mess from the backyard, usually dodging the very angry Alsatian, bitter over his last whipping and wanting to take it out on someone. Sometimes Joel, their son and my uncle, who was 16 at the time, would see that we needed help to escape the dog. He would sneak out to hold him while we picked up the sloppy turds that were left for our fortnightly visit.

Next, we'd have to scrub our grandmother's filthy kitchen inch by inch. But, because the grease on the walls from her fried fish and dumplings was so ingrained, however much we scrubbed, it seemed to make no difference. While she would be there cooking her 'Saturday soup', which consisted of mutton, dumplings, yam and potatoes, with a few kidney beans thrown in to add to the flavour, she would supervise our chores. She'd stand over us, slapping the backs of our heads and telling us we'd missed a bit. We couldn't tell what we'd missed and what we hadn't, so we'd just keep on scrubbing until the dreaded mealtime arrived three hours later. She would then lay the table, often making me sit by Joel, and I hated sitting next to him because at night when everyone was asleep he would occasionally do the same things that my father did to me.

Our times in that house were full of fear, pain and suffering. Most of the time we couldn't even finish our meals because she'd be screaming at us, saying that we hadn't eaten fast enough and that we'd have to starve for the rest of the day. She'd then send us to the room that we shared with Joel. There was a dividing screen across the room; Joel would have one half and Carl and I the other. Joel always managed to bribe Carl with the offer of playing with his old toys if Carl swapped sides with him and let him sleep with me. Because Carl was so innocent, he went along with the idea. Joel would then sexually abuse me, lying all over me with his body that smelled so. He always stank of urine and he wet his bed every single night of the week. A 16-year-old boy wetting himself because he feared his parents so much.

I thought it best to keep our secret because I'd been told to do the same by my father, and I began to believe that my life was supposed to be like that.

Staying at my mother's parents was so different. With Nana and Granddad, we had loads of fun. I can safely say that they have been the only stable people in our lives. We loved it there and would often beg my mother to let us go there every weekend. She'd always tell us that we had to be fair and let our grandparents share us. We didn't understand what she meant but we had no choice but to agree with her. Our lives were full of horror and the only bit of sanity we had was the time we spent with Nana and Granddad. They loved us with all their hearts and most definitely let us know it. We felt safe in their hands: no beatings, no shouting, no abuse whatsoever from either of them – only love and affection, jokes and a lot of laughter. They made us very happy and their home became our little safe haven, a place where we could play naturally without fear of a good kicking for any of the reasons our father or his parents would dream up.

With Nana and Granddad, we could be happy, normal and very playful children. Our trips to Blackpool with them were something that we looked forward to all year long, but especially on the nights leading up to going, when we would hardly sleep for excitement. When finally the morning arrived for us to leave, we were up at four, begging Granddad to get the car started so that we could get started on what seemed the longest journey ever, even though it was only a few hours' drive. Nana would never leave the house without doing her exercises. She'd stand with her back against one corner of the room and ask me to do the same in the opposite corner. Then we'd swing our hips to the beat of Nana's Abba music, mainly keeping in time with each other, but sometimes racing to see which of us could swing our hips the most, and always giggling away like two little girls.

I remember one morning that, while doing my exercise with Nana, I was so happy looking at her beautiful and kind face across the room that the fact that I was on my way to Blackpool and had been looking forward to it all year totally slipped my mind for a few seconds. That is, until Granddad walked into the room, as if he was tired of waiting and probably sick of Carl asking him where we were. 'Come on, Titch,' he said affectionately to Nana, who was so petite, whereas he was a tall, fine figure of a man.

Rays of Sunshine

We then made our way to Blackpool, with Carl and I doing our usual whinging every ten or so minutes. 'Are we there yet? How long is it going to take?' Nana and Granddad would always laugh at us and one of them would say, 'We have an awful lot further to go, darlings. Don't you worry, when we get there we'll have loads of fun, I promise you. It's worth the wait.' Then Granddad would give us his speech on how patience is a virtue. We would listen to his every word. He'd tell us stories about how he'd had to be patient many times while he fought in the war, as his life could have been totally different if he hadn't been. We were so wrapped up in his stories, and he told us so many, that we would be in Blackpool before we knew it.

Our trips to the seaside were a joy from start to finish. First of all, we would grab our deckchairs from the boot of the car and race along the road alongside the beach to our favourite spot. As we always left very early in the morning, we could claim the spot for ourselves. There we would lay out the breakfast that Nana had so clearly lovingly prepared because it flowed with wonderful tastes that could only have come from her kitchen. We'd eat our feast and then tidy things away, before getting ready to move on to our favourite place – the fairground. Given £5 each to do whatever we liked with – and that went a long way back then – we had two or three hours of real fun, especially on the thrilling rides where we would scream with pride, 'Nana, Granddad, look at me!' Nana would smile and wave at us with a tear in her eye, so happy to see us full of joy. Granddad would nod his head and blow a kiss at us.

Once we'd spent our money, we would move on to our walk along the pier. Then at two we'd go for our regular fish and chips at one of the local restaurants across the road from the beach. By now, our hearts would already be turning from happy to sad as we knew that the time was drawing nearer for us to go back to the place that I can only describe as hell. But there was still a couple of hours on the beach before Granddad would say, 'We have to go soon.' With us being obedient children, we'd not say a word to try to change his mind, though I think that our faces said it all. We hated that time of day, and the fact that we had to go home, as well as facing school the following day, often ruined what was one of the best days we'd had all year.

Walking away from the beach to the car with our heads down, we never wanted to look back on our brief happiness. We knew that we had to move forward and hope for the best. At those times, I often wished that I could tell Nana about my father's abuse, but, as he'd warned me that he would shoot both of my grandparents with his friend's gun, I couldn't say a word.

The dream Carl and I shared of going home and Dad being pleased to see that we'd had a wonderful day never came true, because as soon as we got back we always received the same treatment. In fact, it was worse because he was envious of the fact that we'd had fun. We would bring him some Blackpool rock, in the hope that it would stop him harming us, but he was angry that we'd enjoyed ourselves with what I would call our true parents. He would show his jealousy by waking us in the middle of the night to beat us, for instance, because he couldn't find his passport. It was like that for a long time and nothing much seemed to change at all. Our only aid to survival was the knowledge that we had our Nana and Granddad for comfort, love and happiness on alternate weekends.

3

The First Time

On my fifth birthday, my father forced me to take the day off school, as he did most days. He waited until my mother had left for work, put me into a pretty little red dress and told me that he was taking me out for the day. The entire time he kept on assuring me that he had a very big surprise for me. On the way, he explained to me that I'd have to stay with his girlfriend Emma for a while, as he needed to run some errands. It was nothing unusual, as he often left me with her for short periods of time while Mum was at work. Emma seemed to be a nice enough woman, but what I didn't realise at the time was that she was a hooker.

I was very excited, not knowing what we were about to do. I'm going to get a big birthday treat, I was thinking.

But, as the minutes went by, I soon realised that what I was about to experience was quite the opposite. Emma took me with her to see one of her clients. At first, I was curious as to why she'd taken me to a tool shop for my birthday surprise and I was even more baffled when the man there handed her a large sum of money. It quickly became obvious what was going to happen when she took me behind the shop and forced me down on to a workbench. After tying me to this, they shoved a dirty cloth in my mouth. The man paced about the room, then took out some tools from his kit, as I kicked and struggled as much as I could. At the time, I knew that it was wrong, if only because my dad had said that he was the only person on earth allowed to touch me in those places. I was filled with fear and physical pain, not knowing what else he might do to me or if I'd be leaving that place alive.

What I did know is that I needed to get out of there, so I persevered with my battle and eventually Emma gave in, untying me while he was in the toilet. I ran as fast as I could towards the door, but it seemed to be so far away. Running past electrical tools really put the fear of God in me – they always seemed so loud and dangerous. Yet they were not as threatening to me as he was. He was behind me now, so close that I could feel and smell his tobacco-reeking breath on the back of my neck. I was running to that door with all the speed that my tiny legs could summon. I put everything I had into getting out of that shop and away from them. It seemed to take for ever, because with every step that I took he was right there behind me, breathing down my neck, getting closer to me and shouting, 'Stop right now, you little bitch! Stop, you filthy little whore!'

It was a dingy electrical tools store, so cold, dark and grubby, in the middle of a busy high street. No wonder the shop was closed in the middle of the day – he probably never had any customers. He was a scruffy, dirty old man with crooked teeth and ripped trousers without a zip. I'll never forget his face; I've never seen a man so ugly. I could just about see the door now but he was so near I had no choice but to bite him. I can still remember his scream and, when I think about it now, he even sounded like a pervert. I must have torn his skin, because as many times as I tried to brush away the taste I could still taste the dirt from his hands in my mouth days later. As he whimpered in pain, I crawled between his legs and scrambled outside. I couldn't believe my luck when I saw my mum. I blinked, rubbed my eyes and smiled with joy and such relief when I spotted her standing on the other side of the road. There she was, taking her lunch break from work, and saving my life.

In a great panic, I ran to her, totally oblivious to the cars that were coming towards me. Mum screamed at the drivers to stop and I reached her safely. I went straight into great detail about what had just happened to me, wailing and collapsing into her arms. She took me to the local GP, who, after examining me, told her to tell my dad to keep me away from strange men, and sent me home with some antibiotics. Wow, although it seems like yesterday to me, I can see just how different things were back then. That wouldn't happen nowadays; instead, the doctor would call social services straight away.

How I hated taking those antibiotics, but I used to be on them all the time. I know why now, but back then I used to think there was something seriously wrong with me physically. I never thought that it was being caused by my father. No wonder I was a hypochondriac! I always had something wrong with me, even when I was healthy, and even at that age I was always in pain somewhere. I suppose all those vaginal infections didn't help. Mum used to go mad at me for not wiping myself properly when I went to the toilet. 'I'm fed up with taking you to the doctor's, Sara,' she'd say.

That was a line I would hear from her regularly. But, while she was dragging me off to the toilet and showing me how to wipe myself, little did she know that it had nothing at all to do with my personal hygiene. I knew exactly how to use the toilet; if only she could have guessed that it was all down to being left alone with my father and what he was doing to me while she was gone.

When Dad came home, in the middle of the night, Mum told him what had happened with Emma earlier that day and he got very angry. He beat her up severely, hitting her time after time, slapping, kicking and punching her and accusing her, 'Yuh just jealous of Emma.

Yuh have to make tings up feh mess up my shit, yuh jealous bitch.'

I now know that he knew the truth about what they were going to do to me. He must have, because if my kid had run away like I had I would have gone home straight away to check if she was there, but he waited until the middle of the night to come back. He was beating my mother out of guilt, covering his tracks again, trying to protect himself against getting into any trouble, and she paid the price for trying to look after me. How could he? He really scared me. Sometimes I would look at him and wonder if he was the Devil.

He left the house after beating Mum, and she went straight to bed. Carl and I tried to comfort her but we knew that she was in awful pain and all she wanted was to be left alone. Her eyes were bruised, her ribs were badly bruised and she could hardly breathe in. He had really hurt her this time, and we were worried for her health. We all hoped that he would be spending the night at his girlfriend's house but we weren't so lucky. He came home an hour later, very drunk, and my heart sank because I knew what was coming next.

I heard his footsteps on the landing. He was heading for my room and there was nothing that I, or anyone else, could do about it. He dragged me out of the bed by my nightdress, took me downstairs and beat me with the wire from his precious speakers! The only time he would touch them was when he wanted to beat us, but if we touched them we got a beating. He was whipping me because of his love of women and money, just as he had done so many times in the past. He had hit my brother and me quite often for telling Mum about his other women. I always thought that I was doing the right thing by telling her about Dad sleeping with other women. He used to take us to many places and make us sit at the end of the bed while he went to sleep with his girlfriends. That's what he used to call it, but even at our age we knew that he was doing more than sleeping.

Only a few weeks before, he had taken the two of us to Emma's flat, where we had to sit on a deckchair at the end of the bed while it was bouncing up and down and making loads of noise. Then some mice came out of the floorboards and, of course, Carl and I started screaming. Dad jumped out of bed naked and kicked us both in the face. We were silenced straight away, so scared that we cuddled each other and went to sleep. It was the only way we could make the wretched feeling go away: a definite case of mind over matter.

We told Mum what had happened that night and she went crazy at Dad, which resulted in him being very annoyed with us. When she'd gone to work, he made us both stay off school that day. He told us to strip off every single item of clothing and scrub the kitchen floor with a scouring pad and bleach. My knees were sore from the bleach for days afterwards, which is why I wouldn't have told my mother about what had happened with Emma

30

and her client. And, if she hadn't been on the other side of the road on her lunch break at that precise moment, she would never have known what happened. I had certainly learned my lesson! But she was there and she saw me running out of the shop, so I had no choice but to tell her.

She tried to stop my father from beating me for telling her about Emma and that creep, but she got punched in her face and fell to the floor. She quickly gave in as she was in enough pain from the beatings she had received earlier on that day and probably couldn't have taken much more. Mum was very petite, a stunning tiny blonde with beautiful sapphire-blue eyes that were always surrounded by blue and purple eye shadow to cover up her bruises from my father's beatings. Dad was a very large black man who was very intimidating. His eyes were dark and what should have been their whites were yellow, so he looked very evil and very scary.

After he had finished whipping me with the speaker wire, he sent me back to bed. I ran as fast as I could. I knew that, if I hesitated, or cried too loud, he would call me back and hit me again, so I raced to my room and went straight to sleep, hoping and praying that he would leave me alone for the rest of the night. That time he did and at last I got to sleep, tucked up in my duvet.

When I woke up the following morning, Dad told me that I wasn't going to school. Mum kissed me goodbye and went off to work. It was strange: they were both acting as though nothing had happened and the fact that my birthday had been ruined didn't seem to bother them at all. I was surprised at my mother's strength. She'd received a very severe beating the day before but somehow she had managed to use her make-up to hide the results. The previous day, she had looked as if she had been run over by a truck, but now she'd managed to pull it off once more and make herself look beautiful again. That morning, she was gliding around as though she wasn't in any pain, but she must have been. She was obviously doing it for his benefit, to make him feel normal and less guilty.

As soon as she left the house, Dad called out to me to come into the room and lie next to him on the sofa — the sofa he slept on all day every day between drinking his super-strength lagers and smoking his marijuana. My brother had gone to school and I was wishing that my father had let me go too, because he was acting stranger than ever. I thought I knew what to expect from him when he called me to the sofa. But this time it was different.

'Sara, I'm going to show you what that man was going to do to you yesterday,' he said. 'I promise you it won't hurt. Just take off your clothes and lie down.'

I knew that he was going to hurt me. Whether I resisted or not, either way he would hurt me. And whether it was to be a beating or whatever else, he would get his own way, as he had all the power. After all that time of touching me, he had decided that this was the day to cross the line; a time when the word 'father' would go out of the window and the word 'lover' would come into play.

That day was the first time he truly hurt me. Regardless of how many beatings I'd received from him before, he hurt me deeply, which is why I knew at the time that it was wrong. But I also knew that I couldn't do a thing to stop him. I remember thinking, He does this to Mummy, I've seen him. I wonder if it hurts her too. He is scary. I think he wants to kill me. The pain is unbelievable! I held in my screams, fearful that he might kill me, and I almost chewed my lip off. Then I couldn't hold it in any longer. 'Aaah! Mummy, help me, it hurts.'

He looked at me with his evil, cold eyes. 'Go and get dressed and go sit under the stairs.' With a big sigh of relief, I ran to the stairs. If he really believed that sitting there was punishment compared with what he was doing to me, he must have been crazier than I thought! I sat quietly and waited all day for my mother to come home from work. I was sick a few times, yet, showing no sympathy, all he gave me was a bowl to throw up in. I sat and played quietly with the phone, which wasn't connected, but I could hear the radio on it playing. That phone gave me a little bit of comfort, but I still panicked that he might hear me playing with it and come and beat me.

It seemed like days rather than hours before Mum arrived home from work. I was so pleased to see her I could have cried, but I knew not to, as he would have got very angry with me for showing her any emotions. He hated to see us cry is what he used to say. I never understood that at all. I used to ask myself why he tried so hard to make us cry if he hated it so much. The way he put it, if you didn't know him, you'd think that he meant it from a loving father's point of view. But no, he didn't like to see us cry because he knew he was causing the pain that we were suffering. In hindsight, I suppose it was the only time he showed any remorse for his actions.

As soon as my mother walked through the door, he started shouting, 'That girl has been so naughty. Make her eat her dinner and put her straight to bed. I'm going out, I'll see you all later.'

Mum never asked him what I'd done; she never did. She knew that I wasn't a naughty child as a rule, but she would never question his authority. She says now that she was petrified of him. So she wouldn't simply pretend that she'd sent me to bed, just in case he snuck back home to check on us. He'd done that many times before, which is why she knew not to pretend. She'd learned that lesson.

I bolted my dinner and ran off to bed, where I lay thinking about the events of that day, hoping and praying to God that he wouldn't come home that night and do those things to me again. I believed that I would die from the pain if he did. I soon started to wish that I hadn't rushed my dinner, as I couldn't stop throwing up again. I know now it was definitely due to fear, but at the time I thought I had a tummy bug. My hypochondria again!

Mum kept popping in and out to change my bowl and clean me up, but it seemed so pointless because I was so ill that no sooner had she cleaned me up than I was making a mess of myself again. What made it worse was the fact that I felt so ill that I kept on thinking that, if he came home, Mum would tell him how ill I'd been and he would come up to my room to check on me. The fear that he would start touching me and doing again the things that he'd done earlier that day was so immense that, as much as I wanted to stop for that reason, I would throw up time after time.

4

No Way Out

Dad never came to my room that night. It left me wondering if he was angry with me for being ill. I'm not sure what time he came back, but Mum seemed to be in a good mood when she came into my room to wake me in the morning. The only time she would be in a good mood was if he had come back and slept in their bed with her.

Making my way downstairs to get my breakfast, I could smell porridge. I hated porridge, but all that throwing up had made me very hungry and, as much as I disliked it, I had to eat it. Besides, Dad would have killed me if I'd refused. The only thing I could do was hope that the sugar bowl was somewhere near the table, so that I could drown my porridge in sugar to disguise the taste. To my disappointment, it wasn't there. Dad was in the next room and I hoped that he wouldn't hear me whisper, 'Mum, Mum, can I have some sugar, please?'

But he did. I'm sure he used to listen out for us, waiting for an excuse to come in and slap Carl and me around the room. 'Sugar, sugar, weh you want de sugar fa, heh?' He spoke in his West Indian accent; he mostly spoke to us like that when he was very angry. 'Sara, yuh nah go to school and yuh better eat all a yuh porridge too.'

Although I knew that I'd probably throw it all up again, I rushed it down, eating every drop while retching and trying not to let him see. He kept on coming back into the room; it was hardly worth him leaving, he was coming in and out so fast. Pacing up and down, winding himself up, checking my every move, at last he caught me retching. His eyes widened as he pointed at me and shouted, 'Yuh still nah go to school, do yuh hear me?'

His actions left me confused and asking myself why I didn't just eat it without the sugar. I was telling myself, He's going to hurt me again, I know it. Then the dreaded time of day arrived when everyone left the house, leaving me alone with him. So I was overwhelmed with joy when he said, 'Sara, we're going down the bingo hall. Go get dressed.'

I skipped to my room, thinking, Yeah, I like it there, and Dad seems to be much nicer to me when he is around his friends who own the bingo hall. Most of his good friends go there too. They always look after me, they sometimes buy me nice treats; I hope they do today. I just hope he wins, otherwise he'll be in a foul mood, and he'll probably take it out on Carl and me when we get home, like he always does.

I used to hate it when he would get drunk and gamble away the food money, then come home and beat us, as though it was our fault. He often forced Mum to go and ask Nana for money for food. Luckily, Nana always helped us and we would get to eat a decent meal most of the time.

At the bingo hall, I don't know if it was the porridge or the fear of him losing money there, but I was feeling ill again. Desperately wanting to throw up that disgusting stuff that was still lodged in my throat, I started to retch again. Before I knew it, there was a big pool of sick all over the floor of the bingo hall. Dad's face screwed up like a monster's. I knew he was angry with me, but he was putting on his usual act, pretending he cared like a real father. I went along with him and acted as though everything was normal, but the truth of the matter was I knew that when we got home he would beat me again.

'Are you OK, Sara?' asked Shelly, who owned the place.

I remember thinking that if anyone should be angry it should be her. After all, it was her carpet that I'd just spilled my guts all over.

Dad put on his plastic smile again. Then he started with his lies. 'She'll be just fine, Shelly! Don't you worry. I'll take her home feh clean her up.'

I could tell by his tone of voice that he wouldn't be cleaning me up at all. He was angry; I could feel it as he grabbed my hand and dragged me towards the door. Looking back at Shelly, I hoped she would see the fear in my face, but how was she to know what my dad was really like? Everyone loved him; they all thought he was a good man and a loving, responsible father. I suppose they were right: he could be sometimes. I used to enjoy his company when he was drunk at home with Mum. He would sometimes let us have some cider and we would all have a dance around the front room. I loved his Bob Marley records. Sometimes I used to wish that Bob Marley would come out of the speaker and be my dad, thinking just how much I wouldn't mind having him for a dad, because he had such a nice smile. He looked so loving and kind compared with my dad.

While I was daydreaming my way home, my father was dragging me across the high street, tugging at my arm, telling me to hurry because 'You fucking stink like the sewers'. As we approached the estate, I could see our front door in the distance. I started to feel myself wanting to cry, but I knew not to, as Dad would have hit me really hard if I'd dared. The communal hallway looked so long, the stairs so steep and gloomy. I didn't want to go upstairs to the front room. I didn't want to be alone with him in that room ever again, yet I had no choice.

'Sara, go run yourself a bath now, get up dem stairs and tek off yuh clothes,' he said.

No Way Out

I was right: he had no intention of cleaning me up at all, only an evil intention of putting me through more pain, as if, in his eyes, I had done him wrong in a big way. He did the same things to me again and again, telling me that I was naughty and that I deserved it. At the same time, he was also telling me how much he loved me. I was so confused, scared and alone, with nobody to turn to.

Mum would have confronted him if I'd confided in her, but then, I felt sure, he would have killed her. That's the one thing that he promised me he would do if I ever told anyone, which is why I had to keep my secret for so long. It was three more years before he stopped treating me like a lover instead of his little girl. The only reason that he stopped then was because he'd found someone else to abuse. His second cousin, Marie, was a lovely little girl. Her mum rang him out of the blue one day to ask for help. Apparently, her husband had been accused of sexually abusing Marie. She felt that Marie was a handful and didn't want her living with her any more. My mum and dad agreed with her that Marie would be safer coming to stay with us, because she wanted to work at saving her marriage. In fact, both the girl's parents felt that they couldn't do so with her hanging around.

Marie was 13, very vulnerable and in desperate need of someone to trust and confide in, especially as her mother had effectively abandoned her, choosing a paedophile over her own daughter. Dad soon got very close to Marie, mostly by sitting with her and talking about how she felt.

He would always call her dad a 'sick bastard' and ask, 'What kind of a man would do that to his own daughter?' They got so close that one night he came into my room, where she slept, and their relationship progressed from there. I know it sounds shocking but I was happy he'd chosen to have a sexual relationship with Marie, as it meant that he left me alone. The fact that he was sneaking into my room and having sex with her in front of me didn't bother me at all. I was just so glad it wasn't me.

My mother knew that he was creeping out of her bed to be with Marie, but by that point in their relationship she had totally lost her freedom of speech, fearful of the beatings that she got from him whenever she opened her mouth. She couldn't even ask what time it was without him launching into either a verbal or a physical attack. He would accuse her of snooping into his business and tell her, 'You don't ask me anything. Who the fuck do you think you are asking me the time? I'll come in when I like; you can't control me.'

I'm sure my mother never meant it like that but he was so paranoid that he always jumped to conclusions. She knew it was best to keep her mouth shut.

Two years later, Marie fell pregnant with my dad's child. He hadn't touched me at all in that time, but just when I thought it was over Marie decided to go and stay with her sister because she didn't want to rub the fact that she was pregnant in my mum's face. I hoped my dad would leave me alone after she'd gone, but deep down I knew it wouldn't last for long. She had only been gone a few hours when I heard his footsteps creaking on the stairs, coming towards my room. I was lying there frozen stiff, thinking to myself, If I cover my face with my duvet, he just might go away. But my duvet wasn't working. I wanted to die. This is so unfair, I thought. Why didn't Marie stay? Why can't somebody help me?

I had been allowed to go to school every day for the two years Marie was with us, but he came into my room the night after she left and said, 'You have to stay home tomorrow. We're moving home next week and I need your help packing.'

I knew he had no intention of making me help him pack; he had a need to be with me alone, because his other little girl had gone. I was right: he took full advantage of our being alone together the next day. Not a thing was packed when Mum got home from work. Eight hours of abuse is what I endured that day. He said it was because he'd missed me so much. I remember wishing that he'd never stopped abusing me in the first place, because it hurt so much. If he'd not stopped, I wouldn't be in so much pain, I thought. Maybe I would be used to him hurting me like that by now and the pain wouldn't be so bad. When I think about it now, I realise it hurt me more mentally than it did physically, because, just when I thought it was over, it was beginning again.

5

My Father the Monster

Even though we were all living in fear of my father, Carl, little Louise, our baby sister, and I played together a lot while Dad was out at the pub or, more often, at other women's houses. We played as though we were normal, happy children, often forgetting the price we would later pay for our actions. One incident I recall was when Carl and I decided it would be a good idea to play with Mum's tubes of Avon cream. Squirting them at each other and pretending they were our light sabres, we were convinced we were in *Star Wars*. Carl would always play Darth Vader. I ran around the house, trying my hardest to squirt him, hoping I would win the battle. But I was clumsy and kept missing him, ending up leaving greasy marks on my father's precious newly applied blown-vinyl wallpaper.

As soon as we saw the stains, we knew what was to come next. Mum frantically tried to remove them, all the while screaming at us, 'What have you done? He's going to kill me.'

She sent us to bed and we raced upstairs. I lay there with my fingers crossed for hours, praying he wouldn't notice the marks when he came in from drinking. That night, I begged the Lord to make my father blind drunk. I'd heard that phrase many times as a little child and now I hoped it would happen to him. I was desperately hoping to be spared the severe beating that I knew would come if he saw it.

But again my prayers weren't answered, as I heard him shouting, 'Who the fuck put shit 'pon my wall?'

My heart raced so much that I could hear it thumping away inside my chest. I tore across the landing and nudged my brother, whispering, 'Carl, Carl. He's back. Quick, hide.' But we were too late; he was coming up the stairs. Although he weighed only about 12 stone, his footsteps sounded like he was at least 30 stone. He was angry – I could tell by the bang on each and every step. Stupidly, we ducked and tried to run for cover, which always made our fate more severe. We knew that was the worst possible thing we could have done, but it's just a normal reaction when you know that someone is going to beat the living daylights out of you.

He raced across the room towards us – we were crying and shaking with fear by then – grabbed us by the hair and screamed in our faces, 'Which one of you did put cream 'pon my wall?'

We tried to answer, but with each word he tugged our Afros just that little bit harder. I then said, 'Daddy, we were playing.'

What a mistake that was!

He dragged us both downstairs, towards his precious speakers, and asked, 'Which one do you want me to use? The speaker wire? Or my thick leather belt?' He said this while rubbing his hands across his belt with a slight grin on his face. He knew he had won.

He had found yet another excuse to beat us. Not that he needed any. He'd beaten us many times before that night after waking us up in the same manner; often at three o'clock in the morning, because he'd lost his passport. He'd never used it since he left his home country, and he never will. Still, it was an excuse and he used it to full advantage. None of us had ever touched his passport, because he had beaten us so many times over it. But still he would wake us and beat us. I believe he knew where it was, because he always found it the following day, in the same place that he'd left it.

Later, when everyone else had left the house and it was just the two of us alone, he would apologise to me. But he never apologised to Carl; he would pick on him every day for the most trivial of things. He even used the fact that I was better at spelling than Carl, setting up spelling competitions for us. I'd always win and then Carl would get kicked around the room and my father would say, 'How the fuck can she spell better than you? She is one year younger than you, you stupid little fucker.'

I learned over about a year that maybe I should start losing the competitions, as it was too painful to watch my beloved brother get beaten. My father clocked on to what I was doing and then would beat us both. It got to the point where, if he suggested we do a spelling test, we knew what was to come next.

The night when we played with our 'light sabres', we received the most horrific beating we'd ever endured up until that point. He took off all our clothes and wet the speaker wire. He then whipped us three times for every mark that was on the wall. He lashed and thrashed us until one of us owned up to doing the deed. Once I'd confessed, he took his belt off and made Carl watch me take at least thirty lashes. The pain was unbearable, so I screamed my head off, but it didn't faze him at all. He just kept on hitting me time after time, telling me that I was a 'fucking lying little bitch'. My back felt red raw; not an inch of it was left untouched. By the time he stopped, I could hardly walk.

The only reason he stopped was because Louise, who was only a year old at the time, had woken up and started screaming. He raced across the landing to his and my mother's room, where Louise slept. His hands dropped into the cot and he dragged her out by her nightclothes. I couldn't believe what I was seeing when he started slapping her legs while screaming in her face, 'If you don't shut up, I'll take my belt to you, you little shit.'

Naturally, she didn't understand, so he carried out his threat. Although I was in severe pain and weeping because of it, I had suddenly stopped crying for myself and was hurting inside because he was hitting a tiny, defenceless baby. I was five years old and had endured plenty of his beatings, but even then I kept asking myself, how can a man hit a tiny child with little arms and legs?

Fortunately, he didn't hit her for too long. He went to bed after sending Carl and me back upstairs to our rooms. I couldn't walk properly, so Carl helped me back to my room. The entire time he was telling me that he hated him and wanted to go and live with Nana and Granddad. I dreamed of that possibility that night and many nights afterwards. I often wished that, when my mother and father went across to the pub and left the two of us babysitting, they'd get hit by a truck while crossing the dual carriageway, just as my best friend had recently been hit. I often asked myself why an innocent child, a lovely girl, had been taken from this earth. Why was God leaving people like my mother and father here, to torture their kids?

My prayers were never answered; my father kept on playing his games. Enjoying every second of his power trips, he often left us unable to walk properly or wear our clothes on our backs, because they were completely stripped of skin. As his sexual abuse of me became more frequent, he stopped hitting me as often as he used to. He started playing his little games more often with Carl. My brother suffered awfully and in time got to the point where he wouldn't cry because he didn't want to let my father think that he'd won. Eventually, my father lost and stopped hitting Carl, because he knew by the look in his eyes that it was only a matter of time before he would be big enough to fight back. One day, he would be taking a beating from the very person that he had been putting through hell all his life.

My mother started receiving more and more beatings from him, as he was obviously frustrated and needed to lash out at someone. It wasn't until I asked him one day to stop hitting her that he stopped – for at least two years. He told me that, because we had our secret, he'd do anything for me and he was never going to hit her as long as I kept our secret. But not before warning me that, if I told anyone, he would go one step further and kill her. I agreed to keep our secret, not realising that by saying that I'd given him reason to believe that I had no problem with what he was doing to me. He kept on threatening to hit my mother every time I cried after he'd sexually abused me. After a while, I stopped crying and started to bottle it all up. By doing so, I was making it ten times harder for myself to find the courage to go out and get the help I needed from someone. Although I wanted so desperately for him to stop abusing me, I believed that I should carry on so that I could save my mother's life. The ironic thing is, there was nobody there to protect *me*. On the very rare occasions when I was allowed to go to school, my father would be there at the fence that ran along the dual carriageway. He would watch me play with my friends throughout my entire break, often waving at me to let me know that he was there. None of the teachers thought anything of the fact that he was there during every break.

There were times when I hoped he was there watching me. Like the time when a teacher threw me over a chair for copying someone else's work. When that happened, I tried to explain to him that I needed help as I was struggling with my work because of my lack of schooling, but he flipped and started calling me names. I knew that my dad would be there during my break, so I waited patiently. I smiled with absolute joy when I saw him, raced over and spilled it all out as fast as I could. He almost choked on his chocolate bar as he grabbed my arm, then rushed into the school, threatening to kill my teacher. After the longest apology I've ever heard to date, my father was satisfied that the teacher had grovelled enough for him to be able to walk out of the room with his chest stuck out and his head in the air.

He took me straight home and on the way he told me that he already knew what the teacher had done. Apparently, he was on his way in to have him. When he said that he knew my every move and that I couldn't do anything without him knowing, because he could see me all the time, he confirmed my fear that he was some kind of a psychic. The following day, when he sent me to the shop for his cigarettes, I raced off feeling happy to be out of the house alone. I got his cigarettes and on the way back I saw a cute and cuddly cat sitting on a fence. She was so shy that when I tried to call her she kept hiding her face. I stood there for about an hour, forgetting about my father's cigarettes — and my life at home. I cherished every second as the cat got more confident and came towards me. Then it hit me: I'd committed a crime. How dare I not get his precious cigarettes to him within minutes of him asking? I quickly put her down and ran home, my heart thumping in my chest.

When I got there, he was waiting on the doorstep with a grin on his face. I gave him his cigarettes and raced inside. Part of me knew that he was going to beat me but hoped that he wouldn't. As he followed me up the stairs, it seemed that he was only one step behind me. He was loving it: he'd won. Giving out the craziest laugh, chuckling and squealing, he grabbed me by the hair and the games began. 'Didn't I tell you I could see your every move?' My heart raced. I kept on thinking, How does he know what I'm doing? I then asked him and he said, 'You should have left the cat alone and brought me my cigarettes.'

Because I was only a child, I believed him and didn't grasp that he had been watching my every move for a long time. I didn't realise that he was just trying to keep me under his watchful eye so that I couldn't tell anyone about him. All I felt was paranoid that he could always see me. I convinced myself that the only place I was safe from his watchful eye was under my duvet.

6

A New Home

We moved house when I was ten. Dad had seen a new opportunity to fill his pockets, by opening a gambling den. With Mum still at work, we were left to fend for ourselves upstairs while he ran his gambling business in the kitchen. The noise of the loud reggae music and the clouds of smoke billowing up the stairs didn't bother me at all, because I was quite happy to take care of my brothers and sisters and it meant we didn't have to spend too much time around Dad. Carl was at work, as my uncle had given him a part-time job with Mum. He was only 11 at the time yet he loved it, because it meant that he got away from Dad for a few hours.

Carl also loved having the pocket money to spend on his weights, which he was using every day to bulk himself up. He used to say that once he turned 16 he was going to hurt our father for all the times he'd hurt us. He trained hard every day. I think he meant it: he wanted revenge. It's such a shame, and if ever my son felt that way about his own father it would kill me. Carl was only 11, but what a burden he'd had to carry for years.

On one of my father's gambling nights, I noticed that a film was about to come on the TV, so I put the little ones to bed, grabbed my duvet and lay on the sofa with the biscuits that I'd bought with my babysitting money. Ted Danson was in it and I really liked him. I thought that he was fantastic in *Cheers*, a very funny guy. But I soon went off him when I saw that in the film he was doing and saying the same things to his daughter as my father was to me. Her life was almost identical to the life I'd been living for the past five years. Now I truly believed Ted Danson was horrible. That night, I thought to myself, I used to like him but now I think he's a monster, just like my dad. It's so strange how things on TV seem so real when you're a young child.

I was still watching the film when I heard a faint noise in the house and knew I had to rush and change channels as Dad was coming upstairs. But it was too late. His voice echoed as he bellowed at me, 'What kind a film you a tink say you a fuckin' watch hee?' It was his patois again, so I knew he was really angry and I tried to save myself from his violence. 'Daddy, it just...' But, before I could finish the sentence, it was *slap*! 'Don't let me ketch you a watch dem kind a film again, ya hear me. Dem have pervert in a dem.'

I hated him so much! He'd finally broken me down. I totally lost my temper. I wanted to kill him. Then something snapped inside me and I started to shout at him, 'You are a pervert. I'm going downstairs to tell everyone exactly what you're like.'

His eyes widened with anger and disbelief, then he picked me up and started to carry me up the stairs towards my bedroom, telling me that I was out of line. But he was still making me so angry that I wished he was dead. Fuck him, I was thinking. I'm going to kick and scream and that will get someone's attention! I stopped when I saw that look in his eyes. When he gets that look, you can almost see what he's thinking. I could feel myself falling: he'd just dropped me over the banister as though he was a builder getting rid of some debris! Deep down I'd known that was exactly what he was about to do, yet part of me was hoping that he wouldn't.

He's such an evil monster and I don't know where I found the courage to defy him. Perhaps it was because not only had I been through enough suffering at his hands already, but I'd also watched enough of the film to see that his threats were probably idle. Still, I knew not to take it too far because I knew what a violent pig he could be. God, I hated his guts!

The pain from the fall was unbearable. My back felt shattered. I crawled up the stairs, climbed into bed and covered myself with my duvet, praying that a day would come when I could escape the life that had been thrown at me and that I seemed doomed to live out. I begged the Lord to come and save me. Time after time I asked him why he was letting these terrible things happen to me. Every time I reached out my hand to him, he wasn't there, which left me feeling very much alone, because I believed that only God could see what my father was doing to me, and maybe he was the one to save me. When my dreams never came true, I slowly started to lose my faith in God and I'm sure that is why I'm now an atheist.

That night I prayed so hard that I slept for just two or three hours. I cried, begged and pleaded, wishing for something, anything to happen, even a bolt of lightning to strike my father down.

In the morning, my mother asked me why I was so bruised, and I said, 'Mum, I fell down the stairs carrying Louise to bed.' It was the only answer I could give. I wanted to tell her the truth, but in a trice my father had taken any courage that I'd found.

Mum sighed and said, 'Oh, Sara, you should have asked your father to do that.'

As much as I wanted to tell her the truth, his threats from the night before were enough to silence me. Besides, as a child who is brought up to do as you are told or get a beating, you tend to listen to those threats, so I answered with yet another lie: 'Dad was busy, so I tried to help.' I hated lying to my mother, but I felt I had no choice and couldn't tell her the truth.

I had to stay off school that day, because my father told me that he wanted to make sure I was all right. He said he would be taking me shopping as he had seen a new dress in town that he'd been thinking about buying for me. After all the help that I'd given him the night before, I deserved a new dress, he said.

As we walked along the busy high street, he turned to me and said, 'Sara, I'm sorry about what happened last night, but you really frightened me. I don't want to lose you. I love you more than your mother and I would like us to have a baby together.'

My heart was beating faster and faster with his every word. Why me? I asked myself. Why won't he stop saying these things? He's my dad. What is happening to me? I love him and I want him to stop! If only he could stop, I would never tell a soul! I don't think he ever will, he's taken it too far. Besides, he doesn't seem to care about any of us, not like he's supposed to, anyway.

I had just turned 11. My periods had started only two months before. I'd already convinced my mother that I needed to go on the pill. I told her that I was bleeding heavily, so she took me to see the doctor and he prescribed it for me. I only knew to say that because I'd overheard my aunt and my mother talking, but, boy, was I glad that I had listened in on that conversation!

My father wants me to have a baby with him! I was

feeling a great sense of panic and thinking, I must get home and hide my pills. If he sees them, he'll throw them away and more than likely hit me. I know he's trying to convince me that this is right, but I know it's insane. I then decided to start faking super-long periods, putting tomato ketchup in my underwear in case he looked. I didn't know if it would work, but in my desperation I had to do something. There was no way I was going to let my father get me pregnant!

Six months passed. I'd managed to keep him away from me, but he knew that I was up to something, so he decided to make me sleep in the bed with him and my mother. He would send her to get me in the middle of the night. 'Rachel, I haven't seen my favourite little girl for a few days. Could you go and get her? Because I've missed her.'

She always did what he wanted. She wouldn't have known how to say no to him. My mother was obsessed with my father to the point where she even started to show jealousy towards me. She almost always called me 'Daddy's girl', not in an endearing way but in a resentful way, as though she thought that I was taking him away from her. As if she didn't have enough women to worry about without bringing her own daughter into the equation!

At first, I wondered if they were both in on it, and I thought it was because my mother was scared of him. But I started to see a different side to her during those nights that he sent her to get me. She would put me in the bed and within minutes they'd start off with oral sex, then they would have full-on sex. I still don't know to this day if she knew that he was touching me the whole time. Those sickening nights went on for a year. Dad was trying to make me jealous, genuinely believing that I should have been. Little did he know that the two of them were making me stronger. I was slowly coming to the realisation that I had no parents at all! Which was when I started looking for somebody that I felt I could confide in; and, hopefully, that person would help me to escape them both.

7

Almost Caught

I knew that the time to escape my father was drawing even nearer when one day he was on top of me on the sofa and Carl walked in. He quickly jumped off me and shouted at my brother to leave the room. Hours later, when my father had gone to visit one of his many women, Carl asked me if he was sexually abusing me. At that precise moment, I should have felt that my brother had just thrown me a lifeline, but instead I felt nothing but panic and shame. Even though I was already considering trying to escape the reign of terror he was inflicting upon me, I felt numb inside and immediately did what I'd been taught to do, which was lie. Lying became an automatic response for me, so much so that I couldn't even tell the truth when I wanted to, because of the fear that would race around my entire body and then explode inside my head.

Besides, what could Carl do to help me? He was in just as vulnerable a position as I was. Now I was in a panic about him and screamed 'NO!' in his face, in the hope that he would get the message and understand that we would both be dead that very night if he tried to confront my father. Then he told me that he knew that it was happening and the truth would come out one day. I nodded as if to tell him that he was right, and he went back to his weights to build himself up for the day when he would kick our father's arse for every incident that had ever taken place. We never again discussed the fact that he knew.

But my mother had overheard the conversation and promptly told my father, who waited until the middle of the night and then called Carl to his room, where his row of 20 or so belts of different thicknesses hung across the wardrobe door. He grabbed Carl by his shoulders and spun him round to face him, calling him a 'sick bastard', then beat him across the chest with the thickest belt he could find. But, while he was being beaten, my brother refused to cry and stared my father straight in the eyes. Noticing Carl's deadpan expression, my father quickly stopped. And that was when he admitted defeat – not in words, but we all saw then that he could be scared of something. We knew that he knew that it was only a matter of time before his son found the courage to hit back and it would be payback time.

I regularly tried to distract myself from it all, on one occasion going to the phone box across the road from my house and ringing ChildLine to tell them about our neighbour, a lady with three children whose husband had left her because he couldn't take her abusive ways any more. I often heard her children screaming, 'No, Mummy, no,' while she was beating them with all her might, leaving them covered from head to toe in bruises and scars. Her eldest daughter, Vivienne, who was 18, was pregnant, but hid that fact from her mother for seven months until she kicked off the bathroom door one day while her daughter was trying to take a bath and wouldn't open the door so she could get some detergent from the cupboard. That day, she put her naked daughter straight from the bath out into the backyard in the middle of winter. I often used to go and talk to Vivienne when she'd been put out the back, but this time it was different because I had to rescue her from the embarrassment of having a gang of local boys standing around the gate wolf-whistling at her as though she was a monkey being teased at the zoo.

It made me remember a trip to the zoo with my primary school a few years before, and how I felt when all my friends were taunting these monkeys that I thought were very cute. The poor creatures were all lined up, with a wall behind them and a pool in front of them with electrical wires in the water, while my friends teased them for several minutes by acting like monkeys themselves. Finally, they broke one of the monkeys down and it picked up a piece of its dried excrement and threw it at us. It landed right in our teacher's face, breaking her glasses, and we all laughed, making the monkeys even more excited, so that they all started to throw their excrement at us, until we ran away to safety. But now, looking at Vivienne, I realised she had no escape, and even though she was technically an adult she was suffering like a helpless animal at the hands of her mother.

I knew that trying to help her would result in a beating from my father, but by now I didn't care about myself. I dashed indoors and got my duvet and I was running towards her when I fell over and the boys all turned to me and started laughing. I sprang up and started screaming at them, 'You should be ashamed of yourselves. Look at her, she's suffering.' To my surprise, they all walked away and I was left to get on with comforting my friend. Throwing the duvet over her and holding her really tight, I promised that I would get her some help and told her she had to try to escape her mother. She begged me to help her and so I ran across the road to the call box and called ChildLine, and I told them everything that I knew about her mother.

When I got back home, Vivienne's mother was waiting for me in our kitchen with my duvet in her hands. She then started to rip up the only thing that I thought could save me from my father, while screaming in my face, 'You want to help that fucking whore of a daughter of mine, do you? Well, you can come round to my house and clean my toilet right now.'

My father nodded as if to say, 'Go on then', and I followed her out of the door with my head down. While cleaning her downstairs toilet, I had a lot of time to think about what I'd just done. I'd found the courage to ring someone for help. I couldn't believe my strength and felt quite proud of myself. It was then that I realised I could do it for myself very soon.

The following day, Vivienne's mum had a visit from social services, and before long Vivienne got her own flat away from her mother's torture chamber. When I saw her two years later, she'd lost the terrible stammer that she'd had all her life and thanked me for everything. I felt so happy for her that I cried. Part of me felt envious of her. I wished that I'd had as lucky an escape from my father as she'd had from her mother, and that someone similar to me had seen my pain and suffering, just as I'd done with her. I had nobody but myself, though sometimes that isn't so bad; after all, only I knew what to do; only I knew what he was doing to me, because it was our secret, one that I felt obliged to keep, because not only was I ashamed, I was also scared.

I believed that Vivienne had nothing to be ashamed of because there was nothing sexual between her and her mother, but, although I shouldn't have been ashamed, I carried a guilt that was so immense that I would feel burdened by it for a long time to come. So, when I saw Vivienne after those two years, I felt happy for her but ashamed of myself. We didn't discuss what had happened to me or say anything about the day that I saved her life.

Unfortunately, I wasn't so lucky; my father beat me black and blue for interfering in someone else's business, but somehow it didn't bother me, because I knew that I had finally achieved something. And that was another step towards my escape from hell.

8

Planning the Escape

It was July 1987 and over the past few months I'd been sneaking out to the local community centre while Dad was sleeping at his girlfriend's house. I had to choose my times perfectly so that he didn't know what I was up to, because when he was at home I wasn't allowed out of the house. I had made lots of friends but I had to tell each and every one of them to watch out for my dad. I told them that he didn't want me to play outside because he worried terribly about boys taking advantage of me.

They all understood that my father could be so paranoid about local boys trying to ask me for a date. A lot of them even said, 'Well, look at you. I'm not surprised he won't let you out, you're gorgeous.' Because they understood, they would look out for him for me.

They used to think it was fun and treated it like a game of hide and seek. Whenever they saw him walking towards the community centre they'd run into the centre and sneak me out through the back door. If only they'd known the truth: that he would have beaten both Mum and me if he'd ever found out that I was playing outside the house. I was also protecting them, because if he had known that I had any female friends he would probably have tried to get them to play at my house, and who knows what he would have got up to with them. They were all very nice and kind, so I had to protect them. In any case, nobody deserves to go through what I did.

I got very close to a boy named Phil; he was 16 and I was almost 13. Phil listened to me and I could talk to him about anything. I was getting stronger every day. I knew what needed to be done; I just needed to pick the right time to do it. Eventually, I realised that Phil was a trustworthy friend and the one person I could confide in. I knew that he would be more than willing to help me and, besides, my father would never have messed with him. One thing I had come to understand was that my dad only specialised in physical violence towards women and children, and Phil had ten big brothers and eight sisters, who were well known in the area for defending themselves; nobody messed with them. I soon felt as though the day had arrived for me to get the help that I so desperately needed from someone.

One Sunday, my father had decided to play a friendly

game of football at the local park with his gambling pals. Phil and I had gone along separately to watch them play; Phil was standing across the way, pretending not to know me. Dad had just scored a goal, everybody was cheering, and then the thought came to me: this is my opportunity to talk to Phil. Dad has so many friends, and the park is packed, so there's no way they will see us talking now.

So I turned to Phil with a big smile — I always smile when I'm nervous — and said, 'Phil, meet me at the back of my house in ten minutes, please.'

'Sara, watch out, your dad might see us talking,' he warned me.

'I don't fucking care, Phil. Can you meet me? I can't hold it in any longer. I need someone to help me.'

He turned to me with a very serious look on his face. I could see that he was very worried because he'd never seen me like that and had most definitely never heard me talk about my father in that way. 'All right, calm down. I'll see you soon,' he promised.

I ran all the way home and when I arrived Mum was cooking. I was in such a panic that I couldn't look at her. I walked into the kitchen and then straight outside and sat on the fence at the back of the house to wait for Phil. I remember my sense of relief when I saw him walking towards me. But my mood changed very quickly, because he kept on looking over his shoulder, panicking, wondering what was so important that I'd risk being seen with him. My stomach was in knots. I prayed that he would help me. I told him as quickly as possible — I had to, as I wouldn't have been able to spill the words from my mouth if I'd had a chance to reconsider.

'Phil, I have to tell you something, but you must promise me that you won't tell anyone until I need you to. I need your help, but I need to know that I can trust you one hundred per cent. I feel that I can, but you need to promise me that you are willing to help.'

Now he was even more confused. I could tell by his reply. 'I'll do anything for you, Sara, and you know that!' he told me, adding, 'You are scaring me, so can you please tell me what is wrong?'

Sitting there with my fingers crossed behind my back, thinking, You are my only hope, please don't let me down, I told him everything I could without screaming and crying.

'Phil, my father has been raping me, and I need your help to get away from him.'

'What?' he said.

'Phil, please don't make me say it again. I'm finding this very hard already.'

'No, Sara, I heard you. It's just that I am finding it hard to take in.'

'Can you help me, please?'

'Of course I will. What do you need me to do? I'll do anything you want me to do to help you, you know I will.'

'I don't think my mother will help me — well, I'm just not sure, but I must try. I'm going to throw a bag of clothes out of my bedroom window and, if I'm not back in half an hour, get your brothers or call the police. I don't want you to call the police but, if you feel you have to, just do it, please.'

Phil nodded at me, then put his head in his hands. He was in total shock, so I knew I had to move quickly. When I started walking towards the house, I couldn't believe I was finally going to do it. After all those years of suffering at the hands of that monster, I was going to speak out at last. I was shaking so badly my legs were like jelly. As I approached the kitchen I started to feel sick, but I knew I had to go ahead and do it now, because I'd already told Phil. As I opened the door, my mother turned and looked at me. Oh, I hate her too! I thought to myself and, at the same time, Why am I doing this? I'm not even sure I can trust her. She'll probably tell him and I'll get my head kicked in. Oh, God, am I doing the right thing? Come on, Sara! Pull yourself together, you have no choice. Maybe if I keep my fingers crossed and tell her right now, then perhaps she'll help me.

'Mum, I need to tell you something...' I said, to which she snapped back, 'What is it, Sara? I'm very busy preparing a meal for your father and his friends, for after the match.'

The mixed feelings in me of anger and fear were so strong that I was in panic mode, and then I remembered I hadn't packed a bag or anything. Oh, God, what if she doesn't help me? I thought.

I could see her getting fed up with the way I was glaring

at her, then she said irritably, 'Oh, Sara, what is it? Why are you staring at me? Can you hurry up and tell me? I need to get the dinner done.'

Then I lost it and angrily shouted, 'Oh, fuck it! I hate the both of you. I don't care any more if he kills me. Death has got to be better than this life.'

I took a deep breath and out they came, the words that would change everything forever. 'Mum, Dad has been making me have sex with him. Will you help me?'

Suddenly, she came across all concerned. I'd finally grabbed this blind woman's attention. I almost laughed hysterically when she said, 'What? Sara, who have you told about this? What do you want me to do? I'll talk to him, make him stop.'

I was even more confused by this comment, and thought to myself, If it's that easy, she should have done it years ago. What does she mean 'make him stop'? I want him gone. Then I started shouting at her, 'I knew you wouldn't help me. It's OK, because Phil is waiting for me in the backyard. He'll help me. I'm going; I can't stay here any longer. Dad is trying to make me have a baby with him. Are you deaf? And you... well, as for you, you couldn't give a flying fuck, could you?'

She flew into a rage, yelling at me, 'You've told someone? Why? How could you? I could have sorted this out. He's going to kill us all now. You idiot. Oh, my God. Oh, my God.' She was in a panic, the kind I'd seen from her before, when, say, one of us had broken his speaker and she was frantically trying to repair it. Or when she had ironed the creases in his trousers the wrong way or put too much salt in the soup. I thought to myself, There is no way she'll do anything to help me. So I turned to her and said, 'Goodbye, Mum. I can't stay here. He'll kill me, or force me to have a baby.'

Those words made her have a change of heart, and she got on her knees and said, 'OK, Sara, I'll help you, I swear, but you have to give me some time to work out a plan.'

I really didn't like it. She didn't seem to be taking it seriously enough. But I was left with no choice. I had to wait around to see what she would do. It's a big world out there and I wasn't at an age when I was ready to go it alone. I knew I didn't trust my mother, but I had to wait and see what, if anything, she would do to help me. The whole time I kept thinking, If she tells him, he'll probably kill me. I was past caring about dying, and I'd even told her that death had to be better than my present life. Meanwhile, I knew I had to wait and see what she did.

'Mum, I'm going outside to tell Phil,' I said.

She stared at me with a disgusted look on her face, before nodding hesitantly.

I ran out to Phil and started to tell him about our plans, or should I say lack of plans. When I said to him, 'Phil, my mum needs time to plan what to do,' he wasn't pleased at all, but he agreed to go along with us.

'OK, Sara, I don't like this but I promise not to tell

anyone. My sister lives across the way, so every night at nine o'clock flash your bedroom light twice, just to let me know that you are OK. If you don't, I'll go to the police.'

I was so happy that I had him there for me, because I wasn't sure that I would be OK. After all, my mother could have ganged up on me with my father when he arrived home, and I could have been beaten half to death, or worse. Although I was so frightened that I couldn't think straight, I turned to my friend and calmly said, 'Thank you, Phil. I'll speak to you soon. I promise I'll let you know if anything goes wrong.' Reluctantly, I said goodbye, knowing that this was my only option.

While I hated the fact that Mum hadn't helped me more, I suppose I was hoping for a miracle. But, when it came to Mum and Dad, a miracle would never happen. The only thing close to a miracle with my father is the fact that he once did a day's work. He only did so because my uncle was in the fashion business and there were models there for him to drool over. So, even if it wasn't quite a miracle, to get a day's work out of my father was definitely some kind of a feat.

As for my mother, I can't say I trusted her at all, because she would have sacrificed anything to keep her man happy. After all, she abused her parents' goodwill throughout the years by taking their hard-earned cash from them because her husband was taking our food money. She had also changed from a protective mother into someone who would rather let her kids take a beating than either take one herself or get help from the authorities. Sometimes she would even arrange it so that we got a beating just to distract him from beating her. I wasn't sure that I could trust her at all. She'd gone too far, too often, in her desire to protect him.

Come Monday morning, nothing had been said or done. My father had gone out, so I took the opportunity to speak to my mother again. 'Mum, what are you going to do?'

She sent me into a panic when she replied, 'Sara, I have spoken to Grace – she works for social services. Don't worry, I've known her since school. She'll help us.'

I couldn't believe what she had done. I screamed at her, 'Mum, Grace is married to Dad's friend. She might tell him everything and he could tell Dad.'

'Don't worry, she's a professional,' she said. 'There is no way she would do something like that.'

Although I didn't like the idea of Grace telling her partner about our situation and it getting back to my father, I had no choice but to trust them. In any case, I was at the point where I didn't care if he killed me, as it had to be better than the fear that was consuming my mind. Mum told me to pretend that I was having my period, to keep him away from me that week. Fortunately for both of us, it worked.

Days went by and nothing seemed to be done. I was hoping that he would have gone by then but, before I knew it, it was Sunday again. I felt trapped, as though the only contact I had with the outside world was flashing my bedroom light at nine o'clock every night to let Phil know that I was all right.

Then Dad went out for the night, so I took the chance to ask Mum what she was planning to do about the mess we were in. I desperately needed to know, because she seemed to have done nothing at all. Soon I wished that I had never asked! I couldn't believe the plan she had devised, and what was worse was that it had taken her a week to come up with it. She told us all to scratch ourselves all over before Dad came home that night. She said that if he thought we had scabies he would make us all go to see the doctor. It was pretty lame, but we gave it a go and, to my surprise, it worked. He started shouting at her, 'Take them to the fucking doctor's. I don't want mites 'pon my body. You'd better take them in the morning, first thing. Do you hear me? You fucking tramp.'

I couldn't believe our luck. I was smiling inside, thinking to myself, Tomorrow will be a new day and I'll be free of that demon, and I can't wait.

It was a Monday in August, and Dad was on the sofa as usual. Mum had gone into the room to tell him that we were on our way to the doctor's. He told her to hurry up, saying he wanted breakfast by 11. She panicked so much that I wondered if we were going back home afterwards. And would she go through with speaking to social services? Was she rushing so that she could get home quickly and make his breakfast? I still had no trust in her and was very unsure of my future, so I whispered, 'Mum, promise me that you'll help me.'

She looked at me, her eyes full of fear, and shook her head at me, as if to tell me to shut up. Then she told us to hurry and we threw our coats on.

As we were walking away from the house, panic started to take over her mind. Her face was white like snow, her lips blue. It must have been fear, because it was a warm summer's day. Her heart may have been cold, but there was no way she could have felt cold otherwise. She was obviously terrified that he might call her back for something and see a look of terror on her face that would have made him question what she was up to. We turned the corner, out of Dad's sight, and Mum started screaming, 'Quick, run. We can run now, he can't see us from here, so run as fast as you can.'

Once we'd started running, we didn't slow down all the way to the local social services office, which was just a few hundred yards away. We were all shaking and crying with fear and our throats were so dry that we were finding it hard to swallow. My heart and lungs were pumping so fast that it felt like my ribs were about to crack. We had always lived in fear of him, but it had never felt as strong as it did at that moment.

9

Justice is Served?

We were desperate for help and, if we didn't get it from the people we were about to confide in, we knew we couldn't turn back, because by then he would have come to the conclusion that something was wrong. Mum would have had to tell him what I'd said and done, because, if nothing resulted from that trip to social services, my plan was to run away. Yet, even though he hadn't got a clue what we were about to do, we just couldn't believe we'd arrived there safely, we were so scared.

Mum asked the lady on the front desk to put us in a room away from the window, just in case he walked past and saw us. We all had overwhelming feelings of anxiety and disbelief that he hadn't cottoned on to our plans. I suppose, if you live with the Devil, you automatically assume that he knows everything, and to us he was definitely the Devil! But slowly the weight of our shared fear started to lift and the feeling of being in a safe place for the first time in so many years was amazing. We had finally done it. He couldn't hurt us any more.

The receptionist soon realised that Mum's fear was genuine and got us into a room at the back of the offices. As we entered, I started to feel very scared; it was all starting to sink in. I was going to tell everyone what my father had been doing to me. I realised that he would more than likely go to prison, but I didn't know if I could face it. He's my father, I was thinking. How can I do that to him?

As the social worker walked through the door, I started to clam up and I knew I couldn't tell her everything. Even after all my father had done to me, I still didn't want him to be sent down for years. I felt guilty and blamed myself. When she spoke to me, I almost jumped out of my skin. 'Hello, Sara, my name's Jane. I'm here to help you, so please don't worry about a thing. Are you ready to talk to me?'

I wasn't ready at all, but I mumbled, 'Yes.'

She said, 'Sara, you don't have to go into everything with me just yet, but, if you could confirm what your mother has told us, I'll call a lady from the police who can help you. Don't worry, she is very nice, and I can assure you she'll take care of you.'

So now I had to tell them, and I started to whisper, 'My

dad has been making me have sex with him...' I was so numb inside I didn't even feel like crying. I kept on asking myself, What's wrong with me? This is the first time I've told a complete stranger. I'm supposed to be crying. Why can't I?

As the social worker looked at me, I knew she could see from my pained expression that I was dying inside. There she was, looking straight into my eyes. I could see tears in hers. I wondered what she was thinking. At the time, I decided she was probably disgusted with me. I felt so strange. I could see her lips moving but I couldn't hear a thing, because I had too much to think about. I didn't want to discuss it any more. I just wished that I was dead, that I had confronted him with it and he'd killed me. The woman's voice was so faint when she said, 'Sara, Sara. OK, Sara, that's all you need to say for now. I'll call someone to come and speak to you. Wait here, and don't worry, you're safe now.'

I started pacing up and down, panicking and asking my mother questions. 'Mum, why won't they hurry? I hate this waiting. Will they arrest me?'

She snapped at me, 'Arrest you for what, Sara?'

I said, 'For what Dad has been doing. They might think that I let him do it.'

For the first time in years, she sounded like a caring mother when she said, 'Don't worry, it's not your fault. It's him, not you.'

Sitting there feeling helpless and lost, I still couldn't

help feeling guilty and ashamed, thinking, It's not all his fault, it can't be. I must be to blame, otherwise I wouldn't be feeling so ashamed.

Then the police arrived, but by that time I'd decided that I couldn't tell them everything because I was worried they would blame me. They were whispering and looking at me, leaving me asking myself questions again. Why can't they talk in front of me? Why are they being so rude?

They were making me feel so scared, with their suits and uniforms. They all looked so professional and capable of anything. And then one of the women started heading my way. Trapped in that room with only one door, wondering how I could escape, I told myself, I can't do this any more. I want to go home. I've never felt such strong emotions. I feel more trapped than I do around my father. At least I had a way of getting away from him occasionally, but I can't do this with these people now, because it's already gone too far. They know about my father. They will never let this go now, it's far too late. Mum should have done this last week. I was much more prepared then, but now I've had a chance to think about things I wish I'd never told her. Maybe he would have stopped eventually.

By now, I had the biggest lump in my throat, as though I was being strangled and my Adam's apple was about to pop out of my mouth.

Then the policewoman started talking to me. 'Hi, Sara,

Justice is Served?

I'm Karen. I'll need to take a small statement from you now. In your own time, there's no rush, when you're ready. We'll get what you have to say written down, then, if I feel that we need to, I'll send my officers to your house to arrest your dad, if you like. If you'd feel more comfortable at home, we can go there to make a full statement. I think it's better at home for you – you might be able to remember more there.'

We started making the statement, but already I was lying to her. I told her that he had been touching me for two years and then he made me have sex with him six months ago. I also said that he had only made me have sex with him about ten times. I couldn't believe that I was lying, but I suppose that was what I'd been taught to do from a very young age. I then felt that I needed a break as I couldn't handle the pressure, so I asked, 'Can I go to the toilet, please?'

'Yes, of course you can, Sara,' Karen answered.

I just needed time to think. I ran to the toilets, and as I locked the door and checked that nobody was outside I couldn't stop crying, frightened that they would lock me away too. How can I tell the truth? I asked myself. I can't tell them he has been making me have sex with him since I was five, because they'll wonder why I didn't tell them sooner. Plus I've already lied, so I can't tell them the truth now, because then they won't believe me at all. After washing away my tears and drying my face, I stood looking at myself in the mirror.

I wanted to break it and cut myself. I didn't want to be Daddy's pretty little girl any more. I wished so hard that I was ugly. I hated myself!

It took a lot of strength to pull myself away from those thoughts, and from the mirror. But I managed to take myself back to the interview room without breaking anything. As I entered, they were whispering again, and I wished they'd stop, because it was making me nervous.

Then Karen turned to my mother and said, 'Where will he be now?'

Mum burst into floods of tears, her voice was shaky and her face had turned white again. She knew she had to tell Karen where he was, but she had made it obvious that she didn't want to, so her voice wobbled as she turned to the policewoman and said, 'He's at home, probably asleep on the sofa.'

Karen replied calmly, 'OK, Rachel, give us your keys and we'll send some officers to arrest him right away.'

Mum was rifling through her bag, which was full of all sorts of things: dummies, rattles, tissues and so on. She was in such a panic that she couldn't find the keys. As she tipped the contents of her bag out on to the table in floods of tears, Karen gave her a hug and told her that everything would be OK. I was thinking something quite different: She doesn't deserve a hug, she should be arrested too. I'd tell them that if I knew I wouldn't go into care, but I can't, because she is the only parent that I'll have left — once he's been arrested.

Justice is Served?

I had to look at it like this, because at least she didn't make me do those terrible things with her!

Mum calmed down and handed Karen her keys. I couldn't believe it was really happening and asked myself repeatedly why he didn't stop. Karen gave some officers the keys and came back to sit with us. The room was so quiet that I could hear the clock ticking on the wall. Nobody was talking; we all sat there in total silence waiting to hear whether or not he'd been arrested. It all felt so odd. I never, ever thought I'd go through with it and, even though it was now happening, I still didn't believe it. Only half an hour had gone by, but it felt like days. Time's such a strange thing: when you want it to go quickly, it never does and, when you need more of it, it goes so fast. When an officer knocked at the door at last, my heart skipped a beat and I took a very deep breath.

'Come in,' Karen said, and he entered.

'Hi, ma'am, can you step outside the room for a minute?' he asked.

Karen walked out of the room but quickly came back in and, staring straight at my mum, said, 'Rachel, Sara, he is gone. He's now in police custody.'

The first thing that came out of Mum's mouth was: 'Did he resist arrest?'

Karen smiled at her and said, 'No, he was sleeping on the sofa, just like a baby.'

There were big sighs of relief around the room. Carl was shouting, 'He's gone, he's finally gone.'

Karen patted his back sympathetically, knowing exactly what we were going through. 'Right then, grab your things, kids!' she told us. 'We'll get some cars to take you all home.'

On our way back to the house, I started getting very nervous. I still couldn't tell them *everything*. I didn't want him sent down for years; I just wanted him away from me.

We arrived home. I was so terribly nervous that I offered to make the drinks, trying to prolong things, desperate to put off the inevitable. I knew what I had to do, but it's just so hard to tell anyone a big secret, especially a secret that has been kept for so long. I still don't know exactly how long he abused me for. I could have been a newborn, for all I know. The first time he raped me was when I was five, but how long had he been touching me? I don't know. Besides, I still felt that I couldn't tell them the truth because I'd already said that the abuse had only gone on for a short period. Karen must have known that I was stalling for time, because she asked me to go upstairs and sit down with her. I felt scared and anxious and I thought, This is it! I'll have to tell them something!

Once we started, Karen was asking so many questions that I'm surprised I didn't get confused and slip up. She was very calm and very nice to me, very understanding, but because of my shame I couldn't tell the truth, and I couldn't wait for her and the other officers to go. I just wanted to be normal. While telling Karen parts of what happened, I began to feel so angry. I hated him so much! I was truly hurting and I couldn't believe that my own father had hurt me so much. Even the snippets that I revealed were enough to make me think just how unlucky I'd been to be born into such a terrible family.

Hours went by and we'd gone through my statements again and again. When it was time for me to sign them, I considered telling Karen the truth, but I couldn't find the courage to do so. I raced through reading what I'd said, because I didn't want to see all my lies on paper. I just wanted to go to bed and most definitely didn't want to talk about it any more.

As soon as they left, I grabbed Dad's bottle of white rum from the kitchen and ran upstairs. I took Mum's pills out of her drawer, having decided that today was a good day to take my own life. Although I felt much safer by the time I had tucked myself under my duvet, I still wanted to end it all. I didn't want to face my father in court, but I knew that if I didn't kill myself I would have no choice but to do that. I knew Mum would leave me alone for the rest of the night, as she could see I wanted to be alone. She has never been good at affection and always steers clear of us if we're upset, so that left me with plenty of time to kill myself.

The rum tasted disgusting, and it didn't even make me feel drowsy. I thought I'd be asleep within an hour and never wake again, but all it did was make me feel sick.

And the pills didn't work either. I thought a combination of the pills that I had left and my mother's would definitely work, because there were loads of them.

The next thing I knew, Mum was standing over me, shouting, 'Sara, Sara, wake up!' I was really annoyed to find myself very much alive. Apart from a very bad headache, I was fine, but Mum looked really angry as she said, 'What have you been doing, Sara?'

'Mum, shhhh, I've got a headache,' I told her.

She was furious. 'A headache? You bloody idiot, what were you thinking of? Why on earth would you drink that poison and take my pills? You can't kill yourself with those; you know they're to stop me from getting pregnant. You are going to be ill for days.'

I still can't believe I didn't know that they wouldn't work! I knew a lot for a girl of that age, but whether contraceptive pills could kill you if you took a number of them with alcohol was something I'd never thought about. I sat there and wished I'd found something a little stronger and done myself in properly. What didn't help matters was the fact that Mum was throwing a fit, going on and on. 'What am I going to do? If I tell social services, they'll put you in care. Please don't do it again, Sara, please.'

She always threatened me with my being taken into care, and it sounded like a very scary place. I believe if she hadn't made social services out to be so scary I would have gone to them years before I did, but she had managed to make me believe that going into care was even worse than living with my father, so I panicked.

'Mum, I promise I won't do it again. Please don't call them. I'll be good from now on.'

She assured me that she wouldn't tell my social worker and we never again discussed what I'd tried to do that day.

Three days went by after the arrest before Mum thought it was a good idea to go and see my father in prison. She came home crying. He'd told her that he'd only done it once and that he was drunk at the time. As soon as he realised it was me, he said, he apologised and the only reason he made me keep it a secret was because he was so ashamed.

I felt so angry. I hated him for lying and I started to wish that I had told the police everything. He didn't deserve anything less than life. How could he lie like that? OK, he was drunk sometimes, but what about those mornings when he kept me away from school? He was sober most of the time and he knew what he was doing. Anyway, whether he was drunk or not, he always knew exactly what he was doing.

When I asked my mother why she felt the need to go and see him, she replied, 'I had to make sure you were telling me the truth.' Because I was so hurt that she'd been to see my father, I asked, 'Why would you need to do that? You and I both know that. You fucking knew what he was doing to me all along.'

She slapped my face and that was the first time of many

that I felt I knew for a fact that she had always known about the abuse. I felt that her actions proved that she was guilty, and by slapping my face she had shown me her guilt.

As the days went by, we started to live our new lives, without the Devil watching our every move. Things were so different without him around. We almost felt like we were living for the first time ever, and it was so good that I suddenly wanted my dad to get a very long sentence. I didn't want to see him ever again, because life without him was so wonderful.

The day finally arrived for us to go to court, but, even though the police were very supportive, I felt very scared. While waiting to go into the dock and give my evidence, I overheard that he had pleaded guilty. What a relief that was! I really didn't want to stand there and face him, so I was elated. Finally, he was telling the truth. I sat and waited for his sentence to be handed down, smiling inside – until the judge gave him thirty months. Suddenly, I was so angry with myself. If only I'd told the truth, he would have received a much longer sentence. But then I told myself that at least he was away from us, and that this was all that mattered to me at the time.

A few days later, we had our first Christmas without Dad and his other women, who used to take it in turns to stay over at Christmas. As kids, we were excited for years that our brothers and sisters by these women were coming to spend Christmas with us, as we rarely got to see them. It wasn't until we were a bit older that we realised that Dad was making Mum have threesomes with him and his girlfriends Emma and Marisa.

The whole thing would almost always end up in a big fight and there would be an ambulance or the police at the door by around three o'clock in the morning on Boxing Day. Emma and Marisa would attack my mother. When I was ten, Marisa beat her and I tried to stop her. I woke up, heard the screams and ran downstairs with Carl's Bullworker exerciser in my hands. I was fed up with these women hurting my mum. After all, she was his wife, so why were they angry with her when they were the bits on the side?

As I rushed into the room, I saw Marisa on top of my mother, hitting her, while he just stood there with a gigantic grin on his face. He's so sick! He was loving it: two women fighting over him, and he'd caused the entire thing as usual. They were all naked, so it was obvious what had been going on between them. I tried to step in, but I got knocked to the floor and ended up with a black eye. Although the entire left side of my face was throbbing, I persevered and eventually managed to get Marisa out of the house by chasing her down the stairs with my Chihuahua pup Peppy, 'the ankle-biter'. I'd finally managed to get Granddad to buy me a dog and I was so proud of the little chap.

I felt so proud of myself, too, that I'd run her naked

arse all the way out of the estate with Peppy and the Bullworker, which I had to carry in both hands because of the weight of the thing. I didn't care that I could have got hurt even more than I already had, because I was sticking up for my mother and making sure she didn't lose the baby she had been carrying for five months. But it was too late: the damage had been done and the baby died that day.

All those terrible memories of previous Christmases with my father made our first one without him an even more wonderful experience. It was the best Christmas I'd ever had: no more worries about big fights and him sneaking into my room. Everyone enjoyed every second of it, because everything was perfect, and that night we all slept well.

10

Living With it, or Not?

One of my mother's most selfish and despicable acts occurred only two days after my father's arrest. Although I'd been assured by the police officer who dealt with my case that my court appearance wouldn't be for quite a while, I couldn't help worrying about the day when I'd have to face my father in the dock.

I couldn't sleep and after much tossing and turning I went downstairs to get a glass of water, when I heard noises coming from the front room. I went to walk in, but my mother pushed herself up against the door and told me to go back to bed. I asked her if she was OK but she kept shouting, 'Just go back to bed – now.' I knew something was wrong, but I had no choice but to do as she said.

The following morning at the breakfast table, I asked her what was wrong and she said she'd been upset and hadn't wanted me to see her cry. Because of all that had just taken place, her explanation was very believable, so I didn't mention it again until three weeks later when she called me to her room. She was crying again, so I thought the police had released my father. As I looked into her eyes, my concern grew even deeper. She was in total pain and I felt helpless as I asked, 'What's wrong? Please tell me, has Dad been let out of prison?'

I couldn't believe my ears when she said, 'No, I'm pregnant.'

I gasped for air and straight away pleaded with her, 'Mum, please don't keep it. Having Dad's baby right now will cause problems for the court case. He'll love it, but he doesn't deserve to have any more kids. I know it's cruel but please have an abortion.'

My concern soon turned to hatred and anger when she replied, 'No, you've got it all wrong. It's not your dad's, it's your uncle Miller's – he's the father, stupid! How can it be your dad's? I never slept with him once you'd told me what he'd been doing to you – you know I never.'

What she said gave me even more reason to think that an abortion was a good idea. She had also confirmed that she *did* sleep with my dad after I'd told her about his sexual abuse of me: I could tell by the way she said it to me.

I said, 'You are disgusting! How could you? He's already

married to Auntie Jane and has cheated on her with Auntie Cassandra; they have a kid together too. So he already has two kids, who are cousins and sisters. What would this one be to them? Oh, sorry, the same, yes, cousin, sister or brother, and what would we be? Hmmm, I'm all confused now. You make me sick. You're a whore.'

She tried to avoid any more shame by saying, 'I'm sorry but you know that night when you thought I was upset, I was, but your uncle was with me. He consoled me and one thing led to another. I haven't even told him, I will never have to, because I'm going to have an abortion.'

She hadn't realised it but she'd just made things a whole lot worse by telling me that she had already come to a decision about having an abortion, so I said to her, 'Then why did you feel the need to tell me anything? I didn't need to know at all: you could have just gone and done it and not told a soul.'

Then came the pathetic excuses. 'Well, I needed to tell someone. I couldn't keep it to myself, and who else could I have told? Not one person around here would respect me if I told them this.'

There she was again: more concerned about how her friends would feel than how badly it would affect her daughter, who was already dying inside because she felt like she'd lost everything.

She went ahead with the abortion, but just when I thought it was all behind us she told me she had fallen in love with another of Dad's friends, and this time she was blatant about it. He lived a few doors away from our house. She started to get me to watch the kids while she went round to his house late at night and she would come home in the early hours of the morning, making it obvious that they were sleeping together. Before long, she fell pregnant by him, too, and abortion to her became just another form of contraception.

And it wasn't long either before I started to act pretty much the same as her. I had many boyfriends in a short period of time, believing in my heart of hearts that behaving like this was the way forward, the only way to get over my abuse, because my mother certainly wasn't helping me. I quickly got myself a name on the estate. I was officially the young slapper of the area and many boys thought they could get into my knickers. At the time, Mum seemed very pleased with my behaviour. As soon as she knew that I'd had sex with boys, she started asking me to go to blues parties with her almost every night of the week to pull blokes. By the time I was 15, I'd spent more time at blues parties than I had at school in my entire life. Mum didn't seem to mind the fact that I was bringing men back to the house and if I wanted them to stay over it was my choice. No rules at all were ever laid down.

After a while, Mum calmed down, started to stay at home more often and even seemed to be behaving like a responsible mother. She had only started doing so because she'd started dating another of Dad's friends and this time it was serious. He was also the first person she was dating that I totally approved of. I was glad they had got together. Terry had always treated me really well. Even when my father was around, he used to come around to the house and ask my father if he could take me out for the day with his sons. He took me out quite a lot from such a young age that he was one of the few people who could tease me with, 'Don't you give me any lip. I used to change your nappies when you were a baby.'

Terry had consistently taken care of me and we developed a very close relationship. I looked up to him and had the utmost respect for him. He was so caring he even tried to talk to me about my sexual behaviour, but by that point I was too far gone, too wrapped up in my little bubble, just waiting for someone to burst it so that I could come back down to earth. But that bubble was never popped, so things just got worse and worse – until I decided that enough was enough, that I was the only person who could put a stop to my behaviour.

Meanwhile, I carried on getting used and abused by much older men. And one of them was the same uncle that my mum fell pregnant by, who tried to get me to sleep with him too. A lot of men in the area tried to use my pain for their own selfish ends. I suppose in a way I was partly to blame because, if I'd behaved properly, they wouldn't have thought of trying to get me to sleep with them. But they were grown men and should have known better than to take advantage of such a young girl, who was obviously hurting inside and lashing out the only way she knew how. I also believe that I should have had strong people behind me, supporting me, telling me to behave and understanding that the reason that I was acting out was my father's abuse and the fact that I didn't know how to handle it. I was what some would call a lost little girl, looking for someone, anyone, to come along and rescue me. There were many times when I would pray to God for my mother's help, often begging him to take the blindfold from her eyes and make her see me, see my pain, my fear and desperate need for her help and support, for once.

With a constant need for my mother to show me that she cared, there were many times when I would try to get her attention by any means necessary, but to no avail. When I was 15, two years after my dad had gone to prison, I remember feeling very low and my need for her to see my pain was so intense that I stooped as low as to fake a cancer scare. I walked into her bedroom one evening looking at and groping my breast in front of her, hoping she would notice me and say something to make me feel that she cared. I thought I'd get more attention that way, but as I noticed the blank look on her face I knew I had to go one step further and tell her I'd actually found a lump. My heart sank and I started to wish that what I was saying was true when she looked at me and said, 'Well, you'd better make yourself an appointment with the doctor then, hadn't you?'

To have any hope of getting her attention I had to go

through with it. But I felt so silly telling my GP lies when he knew there was nothing wrong with me. I could tell that by the scowl on his face, but I kept on insisting that there was and eventually he gave in to my demands and arranged an appointment at the local clinic for me to have further tests.

Weeks later, I woke up on the day of my appointment, still craving my mother's concern and expecting her to come with me. I went into her room and began to sort out her clothes. Then I grabbed her iron and started to press them in front of her, while asking her to wake up. 'Mum, I've run you a bath. If you don't get up now, we'll be late for my appointment.' My heart dropped into the pit of my stomach when she looked up and said, 'You don't need me to come with you. It's only down the road.'

Thoughts raced around in my head. She doesn't get it, does she? Why can't she see I need her so badly? I was a hurt little girl with so many issues that needed addressing, trying a lot of the time to stay strong so that she didn't have to face the fact that she'd not been the mother she should have been. But, looking back, I'm sure she believed there was nothing wrong with her parenting.

Mum soon fell pregnant by Terry. At last, she was settling down and seemed to be very happy. Terry and I were closer than ever by now, to the point where I felt comfortable with him and had started to call him Dad. For some time, he had been trying to get me to realise that there was more to life than boys and to help me find a direction. I was too young to get a day job, he said. At the same time, he knew that school was no longer an option as I'd changed schools so many times and I'd walked out of my most recent one, where I'd had such a hard time with the other kids' cruelty. Some of them were spreading nasty rumours about me. One story was awful: Carl and I were sleeping with each other and had caught Aids from our father. They then said that Carl had passed it on to my mum. I couldn't take it, so with help from my Nana I got out of going to school. Although she has strong views on a child's need for a good education, she helped me explain to Mum and the school that I couldn't learn anything under those circumstances and that it was best for me to stay at home. The school agreed and I never went in again.

That was when Terry suggested that modelling would be a very good distraction from my troubles. My mum agreed to ask my uncle Tom, her sister's husband, to get some photos done by a friend of his. Sure enough, within a week I was on my way to my first photo session. With Nana as my chaperone, I headed there, still not sure who I was about to meet or even why I was going along with Terry's idea. I felt like a little girl again, holding Nana's hand and asking her lots of questions. 'Nana, what are their names again?'

'Andrew and Lisa,' she replied. 'Andrew is the photographer and Lisa is his girlfriend, and she is also a make-up artist. Your mother has met them and says they're very nice people.'

'I'm ever so excited, Nana.'

'I know, darling, I can't wait to see you all dolled up.'

As we walked into the house, they introduced themselves, and they *were* very nice people. It was a shame they were on such a very busy schedule, as I wanted to go on talking to them because they were so interesting. Lisa started my make-up straight away, while Andrew was in the studio setting up the lights. We ended up having a very successful shoot and I couldn't wait to do more. They had definitely made me think seriously about a modelling career. I loved it and would be looking for an agent once I got my prints back.

After managing to get taken on by a very reputable modelling agency in my hometown, I was working all the time. Since meeting Andrew and Lisa, I was meeting lots of new people and going to nightclubs with them. Sometimes Phil came along with us and we always had fun, but I would usually end up leaving the club before everyone else to have sex with some man I'd just met. I knew that everyone was worried about me but I didn't care. The way I saw it was that they should have been worrying about me years ago, when I really needed them. I'd decided I didn't need them any more. I was a teenager and earning my own money, and I could spend it how I liked.

Blokes were dropping me off at all hours – most times I couldn't even remember their names – and I was spending a lot of time in the bath trying to make myself feel clean after what I'd just done. So much for Terry's idea of getting me into modelling. All that had done was give me a wider circle of people to meet and made me look time after time for comfort in a stranger's arms.

Mum was about to have her baby, so I started thinking about staying at home more to look after her. In fact, I was due to take a month off to do just that, but there was one more job that I'd promised to do with Andrew and Lisa first.

The morning after yet another night out, I looked terrible as Nana and I made our way to my last photo session for a while. Nana kept on saying how pale I was. I said nothing, afraid to tell her where I'd been the night before. I walked along quietly, hoping Lisa would be able to work her magic with the make-up and get rid of those bin-liners underneath my eyes. As we walked in, I whispered in Lisa's ear straight away that I didn't feel too good. She was pleased to hear it and said, 'Andrew is feeling a bit under the weather too. Shall we postpone it for another day?'

'Yes, if you don't mind, Lisa. That would be great,' I replied.

She smiled at me and said, 'OK, Sara, I'll put the kettle on and you can fill me in on your night out.'

I couldn't tell them everything because Nana was under the illusion that I was a little angel. Besides, she looked stunned enough just to hear that I'd been out and I could never have upset her by letting her know what her little angel was really like. Fortunately, I was saved by a knock at the door that prevented me from letting Nana down.

In walked Timmy and I knew immediately that he was the one. He lit up the room and seemed so worldly, with the look of a gangster, thuggish and roguish, about him that really appealed to me at the time. I sat there gazing at him and thinking, I'm in love. It seems so silly when I look back on it now, but at the time it was a big milestone for me because I'd never felt that way before. I'd often thought I did, but I'd been kidding myself to think that the men I'd slept with cared about me, and even if one did I would treat him terribly. I felt a lot of hatred towards men and even while looking for love and hugs I was making them pay for my past. It was a very strange way of dealing with what had happened to me, but that was all I knew then, because not one person had told me it could be any other way.

Lisa got my attention for a while by introducing us. 'Sara, this is Timmy, Matthew and Carlos – they're all in the music business. Timmy has a recording deal, so look out for his album. What will you be calling it, Timmy?'

'Don't know yet, babe, we haven't decided,' Timmy told her.

I was so excited, totally smitten. I'd never met anyone with a music studio (Timmy had built his own studio out of his advance from the record label), who'd met loads of famous people. I'm sure Nana could see it in my eyes, as she knew me better than I thought. She took one look at me and said, 'Right then, if you're not going to be working today, we'd better be off.'

What she didn't account for was the fact that Timmy would drop us home. 'I've got to head off soon, so I'll give you a lift if you like,' he offered.

Nana couldn't refuse when Lisa jumped in and said, 'Oh, that will be nice, Nana. Don't worry, they are nice guys – most of the time.' Which of course pleased me.

We dropped Nana at her house, then I had to direct them, but I was so naive at the time that I didn't even know my way home. I took them on the same route as the bus, which was the long way round but the only route I knew.

Timmy laughed when we got to my house, and said, 'If you wanted to spend more time with me, you should have said. I could have got us here ten minutes ago. I know this area well; it's only round the corner from my house.' He was so cocky.

I was very embarrassed, but I pretended that I'd done it on purpose by saying, 'Yes, I didn't want to go home.'

He laughed again, while turning to his mates and winking.

I asked them to come in for a cup of tea and they accepted. I didn't want Timmy to go. I wanted him to stay with me forever. I knew that Mum wouldn't mind that I'd taken strangers into the house once she knew they were friends of Andew and Lisa. Besides, she hadn't minded when I'd taken so many different men back there in the past.

Living With it, or Not?

Mum acted shy, panicking slightly, running around looking for mugs for our tea. We all talked for a while about nothing much but, as they were about to leave, Timmy handed me his phone number at his studio and asked me for my mine. Then he asked me. 'Would you like to go out for a drink sometime?'

My heart raced as I was thinking, Yes! Yes! He's asked me to go out with him. But then I remembered that Mum would be needing my help at home. I sighed, looked at Timmy and said, 'I can, but you'll have to ring me in about 18 days. Mum is booked in for a Caesarean section in a few days' time and I will have to look after her for at least ten days afterwards.'

He was fine with it and said he couldn't wait. Nor could I. But I tried to play it cool.

The days went by so slowly. I couldn't get Timmy out of my mind. Mum had the baby and came home and they were both doing fine. Finally, the eighteenth day arrived and I sat by the phone as much as I could, hoping he would call me. When it rang, I was so excited that I nearly broke it trying to pick it up.

'Hello, is that Sara?' he said.

'Yes, it is.'

'I bet you thought I'd forgotten about you, didn't you?'

'No, but *I* had.' There I was, trying to play it cool, but the truth of the matter was I was so excited that I almost choked on my sausage roll.

He then made me feel very nervous when he said, 'Could

I speak to your mum, please?' This baffled me a little, but I quickly passed her the phone. Mum pulled her confused face, though her expression soon turned into a smile when he said, 'Hello, Rachel, congratulations on the baby. I'd like to ask you if I can steal your daughter away from you for the evening. I'd like to take her out for a meal.'

'Yes, of course you can, but you'd better look after her, or you'll have me to deal with,' she joked. She was really flattered that he was the type to think to ask her permission, because most guys that I'd introduced her to were very rude. She thought he was charming.

Mum handed the phone back to me and Timmy said, 'If you would like to come out, I will pick you up at seven.'

'OK, I'll be ready for seven,' I replied coolly. 'See you then, bye.' I was trying to stay calm, but I had butterflies. Wow, I thought. I'm going out on a real date.

It took me hours to get ready and, by the time the doorbell rang, I was so nervous that I started questioning my mother, 'How do I look, Mum?'

'You look great. Stop panicking,' she said, laughing.

She opened the door and I could see a big smile on her face when Timmy said, 'Hello, congratulations again on the birth of your son, Rachel. These are for you.' He handed her a huge bunch of flowers.

Mum was in shock and kept on winking at me with a gigantic grin on her face. I knew that she liked him, which was a bonus for me, because already I had a real soft spot for him.

Living With it, or Not?

He opened the car door for me, then drove me to a posh restaurant in the city centre. I had never been to a restaurant before, and going with Timmy made the occasion even more special, with him constantly asking me if everything was fine. We were having a fantastic time, but it was getting late, so he asked, 'Would you like to see the studio on the way home?'

In the hope that he wanted to do a lot more than just show me his mixing desk and so on, I quickly replied, 'Yes, that sounds like a good idea.'

As we walked around the studio, with Timmy showing me photos on the wall of people he had met and worked with, I wasn't really that interested. I just wanted to kiss him. I couldn't wait a second longer, so I made the first move and was so pleased when he responded. I can still remember that moment as though it was yesterday. I felt so emotionally drained that I started crying. For as long as possible I hid my tears, but when we started to make love I couldn't conceal them any longer. Timmy noticed, pulled away from me and asked, 'What's the matter, babe? Am I hurting you?'

I felt so stupid. I didn't know what to say to him, so I told him it was my first proper time.

He couldn't understand what I meant and asked, 'How do you mean, Sara?'

Now I had to tell him everything about my father and my past. I felt I couldn't lie. I thought he needed to know, because I didn't want him to think I was just a kid.

I was, of course, but at the time I thought I was a grown-up. I told him, 'Timmy, my father sexually abused me. He'd done it since I was a baby and it's only been a couple of years since he went to prison. I have behaved terribly since he left but you are the first person I've felt anything for.'

The way he looked at me, I thought he would throw me out of the studio, but his anger wasn't aimed at me: he was furious with my father and wanted to kill him. 'Where is he? The nonce. Just give me his address and I'll send some of the boys around to kill the cunt.'

I didn't want him to do that because Dad had only just finished his sentence and I knew that he knew where we lived. Although we'd moved home since he'd gone, his father had driven his bus past our new house and seen us playing outside and told my father. Dad then wrote a letter to me and one to my mum. He asked me why I'd lied and he denied the entire thing. He said I shouldn't have done what I did to my own father and that he would forgive me if I told the truth.

Mum's letter was pretty much the same, only he told her she shouldn't divorce him because he was a good man and he didn't deserve to be treated the way he had been. He was obviously in a world of his own, clearly in denial, which put the fear of God into both my mother and myself. So Timmy sending his boys around to beat him up wouldn't have taken away our fear. I knew that when he said, 'My boys will kill him,' it only meant a beating, because not many people are capable of premeditated murder. They may have hospitalised him for a while but he would have come looking for us as soon as his wounds had healed.

I begged Timmy to leave it, by telling him the whole story, but knowing my life story and all the pain my father had inflicted on me only made him feel worse. In the end, I had to refuse to give him Dad's address and I truly believe that by doing so I prevented him from carrying out his idea.

After that night, I spent a lot of time with Timmy. Part of me wished that I hadn't told him about my father, because I wasn't sure if he was being so nice to me because he thought that I was vulnerable, which I know now that I was, although at the time I thought I could take on the world.

Months went by and everything was going fine until I got a phone call out of the blue. It was Timmy's girlfriend of 15 years. She asked me if I knew how old he was, because he'd always lied to girls that he'd picked up. He was ten years older than he'd said, she told me. It was bad enough to think that he was 28, but then to hear that he was older than my father and had a partner and a child devastated me. I broke down. The first man I'd fallen in love with had broken my heart, lied to me and made me feel dirty again for sleeping with an old man.

Timmy came to my house about an hour after I'd received the call. He invited me outside to the car to talk, then asked me to go to London with him and stay for a while with a friend of his. He said that the phone call was from his neurotic ex-partner and he didn't want to tell me about her, because he didn't want to frighten me. I believed every single word and my tears dried up within seconds. I hugged him, kissed him and smiled. I couldn't believe he still wanted me after I'd stood there blubbering like a spoiled child, but he did and we started making plans for the future. I suddenly felt more grown-up than I ever had before.

We asked my mum if it was OK for us to go away together and she agreed, on condition that he took me to some modelling agencies while we were in London. We promised her we would do that, then I grabbed a few of my belongings and my portfolio and off we went.

In London, we had a fantastic time, going out to clubs almost every night. I met lots of famous people on the music scene and Timmy got some work for me doing video shoots for some of his friends. I was so pleased to be asked to work for these well-known names. After working and partying hard for weeks, I got into the Storm modelling agency. I couldn't believe I'd been taken on by a top agency, especially as they'd had no more than a quick glimpse of me and hadn't looked at my portfolio at all. I never had much confidence, always thinking that I wasn't good enough. Because of this, I hadn't wanted to go into modelling at all at first. But I had, and now I was there working my way to the top.

Living With it, or Not?

Yet, after a month, I was feeling homesick. Besides, I'd conquered my hometown and London and I wanted to go to the North to find an agent there too. I'd been told that it was best to have at least three agents, to see which one worked best for me. I couldn't wait to get back home with all my cheques from the dozens of jobs I'd done. When I put it to Timmy that I was homesick, he agreed straight away to take me back.

11

Going North

I was pleased to be back home – Mum and I were spending our time looking for the best agent I could get in the North of England. We agreed on the same agency after a long think about their potential to get me lots of work, and booked an appointment for the following Saturday morning. When the time came, we went along, keeping our fingers crossed the whole time. But we didn't need to, because they took one look at me and immediately asked me to return the following week to stay for a while. They explained that they needed their models to live with them up there because they ran training classes in their studio during the week and it made more sense financially for the models to stay with them while they trained. Then they showed us how the agency was run and how they would be training me for a full-time career as a model.

Mum agreed that to get the full benefit from the training I would have to stay at the models' house. In any case, at that time I was waiting for a lot of cheques from my agent in my home town and without those we couldn't really afford for me to travel so often.

My new agent, Leon, offered to take Mum and me to look at the house on the other side of the city. It looked fantastic. I had never seen such a big and beautiful house and I couldn't wait to go back the following week and stay. Mum liked it too and kept saying, 'They must be a reputable agency with that kind of money behind them.'

Leon said that he had seen so many girls in the business who had been taken advantage of that he thought by opening his own agency he could make a difference. Mum liked him and she wanted me on their books, so she signed the paperwork and we went home.

The following Saturday, I went back up there. When I told Timmy that I would be going away for a few weeks, possibly months, he wasn't pleased, but he knew how much my career meant to me.

As I said my goodbyes and made my way to the train station, I felt all grown-up. Later, when I arrived at the agency, I said to myself, Wow, they're all so friendly. The girls are nothing like the models from my hometown and London – they're very helpful.

Leon called me into the office and started showing me

the ropes. 'Hi, Sara, I've asked Andrea to take care of you today. She'll take you back to the house so that you can unpack and freshen up. If you need anything, ask her.'

He handed Andrea the keys to his flash sporty Toyota and we set off for the house, the entire time my thoughts being, This is wonderful. It's like a dream come true, a new life, and I've just left all my troubles behind me back home. I liked London but it was all too fast for me. The North was much more laidback.

A week had gone by and I'd been training very hard each day. Leon noticed my hard work and offered me a photo session with a well-known local photographer. I was so thrilled that, of all the girls in the agency, he had picked me out. I ran to the nearest phone box to call Timmy, so excited I couldn't get my money in the slot fast enough. The phone had only rung twice before Timmy answered.

'Hello, Timmy, it's Sara,' I said.

I knew something was wrong when he replied, 'Hi, Sara. Before you say anything, I've got something to tell you.'

Hesitantly, I asked him, 'What's wrong, Timmy?' I knew deep down what he was about to say, yet I hoped I was wrong.

'I'm going back to my ex, Sara. You shouldn't have left me right now. I'm going through hell with my record deal and, well, she has been there for me.'

I dropped the phone: I didn't want to hear any more. I started screaming and, as I ran back to the agency, cars were swerving all around me, but I didn't care. I was in too much pain. My heart was broken in two.

Dragging myself up the stairs to the office, I decided I wanted to go home and went in to tell Leon that I was leaving, but Andrea was in my way at the door and asked, 'Sara, what's wrong?'

As I tried to explain, I could hardly believe what I was telling her. 'Andrea, he has just dumped me.'

She looked at me with confusion on her face and said, '*Who* has dumped you?'

'My boyfriend has just told me we're finished. I need to go home to talk to him.'

I was so embarrassed, I needed to be alone, but then to make matters worse Leon came out of the office and said, 'Come into my office, please, Sara. Andrea, you too.'

Thoughts were racing around my head: I can't believe this. Why today of all days? Timmy could have spoken to me about this, but he had to choose today. I was happy ten minutes ago and now this. I bet Leon is going to give me a right telling-off!

'Sara, sit down. Andrea, what's going on?' Leon said.

Andrea tried to explain the situation to him. 'Leon, Sara is having a few personal problems and she would like to go home.'

'What kind of problems?' Leon asked me.

I sobbed my heart out as I told him, 'My boyfriend has just dumped me.'

He looked at me with disgust, shook his head and said,

Going North

'Now, Sara, please think about what you are planning to do. You're only 15, with a very bright future ahead of you. You can always meet new people, but this — your career — is happening now. It's something you can't put on hold: models don't get that opportunity. It's not a long-term career. I think you should grab it while you can. Don't worry about men, not at your age.'

No one had ever spoken to me that sensibly before: I'd always been left to do exactly what I wanted, so I told him, 'You are right, Leon. Thank you.'

He asked, 'Does this mean you're staying with us, then?'

He looked very pleased when I smiled at him and said, 'Yes, thank you for your help.' Then he bashed the palm of his hand down on his desk with delight, smiled at the two of us and said, 'Andrea, take Sara home to freshen up. We'll take her out with some of the girls tonight to cheer her up.'

Andrea winked at him and said, 'OK, Leon, we'll see you later. Bye.'

I felt very special that day. They were being so nice to me that I looked up to them and felt a great deal of trust and respect for both Leon and Andrea.

That evening, we went to an expensive hotel for dinner. Leon sent some of the girls from the agency to the pizza place across the road. He said that he was taking his special girls out for some posh nosh. I thought that was a bit rude, but Andrea explained to me that we all took it in turns to go to the posh hotel and the pizza place and that it was the other girls' turn, so then I thought that he was a funny guy. We walked to our table, where a friend of Leon's was waiting. He stood up and Leon introduced us.

'Shall we all sit down and order?' said Leon. 'I'm fucking starving.'

There were four of us girls from the agency, including Andrea, but for some reason Leon's friend was very interested in me. When he asked me if he could read my palm, I replied, 'Yes, I've never had my palm read before.'

He took my hand and stared at it for a minute, then said, 'You're going to live a long time. You'll be very successful in your modelling career. I can see here that you'll never have children.'

Those words freaked me out. Even though I'd never wanted children – my reasoning was that Mum had had so many and I'd raised them all with her and felt I'd had my fill of kids – I snapped at him, 'What? Why not?'

He answered, 'I can't see any children in your palm; you won't have any. I can guarantee it. Come back to me in 20 years' time. I don't think I'm wrong, but, if you don't believe me, or if you've had any by then, I will give you a million pounds.'

He won't even be around in 20 years, I thought. He looks far too old! Then it came to me: he could be right about the children. What if my father's sexual abuse has damaged me internally? What if I can't have babies because of him? I burst into tears again and everyone was asking me what was wrong. I needed to let it out; I couldn't hold it in any longer. I hardly ever got a chance to talk about what my father did to me. Mum always said that she didn't want to discuss it.

As I began to tell them, they all sat there in amazement and when I'd finished they told me how strong I must have been to come through it all. I hated that. If only they knew that I was hurting so bad inside and that all I wanted was my dad to talk to, but I couldn't have a father in my life ever again. I wasn't strong at all, just putting on a brave front for other people so that they didn't have to feel sorry for me.

Leon offered to take me home. He turned to Andrea and said, 'Andrea, you and I will take Sara back. It's very late and she's upset.' Then he turned to his friend and said, 'Could you settle the bill and bring the girls back later? I'll sort you out tomorrow.'

He nodded, winked at them and said, 'Yes, don't you worry about the bill, but remember you owe me one.'

On the way home, I don't know why but I couldn't stop talking to Andrea and Leon about my past. They were really good listeners and seemed to have an extraordinary awareness of my thoughts and the pain I was in. They were such a comfort to me, and some of their advice seemed so valuable that I took care not to miss any point they made. I knew already that Leon could be flippant at times, but even he took it seriously and talked me through my feelings. He offered me a herbal sleeping tablet to calm me down and help me to sleep, but he said that he had to call my mother first to check that she didn't mind.

Back at the house, Leon and Andrea got on the phone to Mum. I hoped she'd say yes as I really needed to sleep: I had a big day ahead of me. Andrea walked in with a smile on her face and said, 'Your mum has agreed to let you take it. You go and take a nice hot bath while I sort you out a glass of wine and your tablet.' That sounded like a great idea.

Then Leon said to me, 'Sara, did I tell you that it's house rules for the girls to not wear underwear to bed? It's not very hygienic. I think it's disgusting myself.'

I nodded but was surprised at the same time, as we never had any rules at home. I thought, They are not only teaching me how to be a model, but they are interested in how I grow up too. Mum has never been interested in our personal hygiene. They're really nice people.

'Goodnight, Leon. Goodnight, Andrea,' I said. 'I'll see you in the morning.'

'OK, Sara, Andrea will bring up your tablet in a minute,' Leon replied.

After my bath, I climbed into bed, waiting for my tablet and wine, then, within seconds and almost as if they knew exactly when to enter the room, in they both walked, and Andrea said, 'Hi, Sara, take this and drink your wine and you'll be out like a light in no time at all.'

I took my tablet and straight away I could feel my eyelids getting heavy. I couldn't even hold my glass of wine, so Andrea had to take it from me. She patted my head and wished me goodnight.

The following morning, I woke up to the loudest-ticking clock in the world. My head felt so heavy I could hardly lift it off the pillow. It was ten o'clock and I couldn't believe that nobody had called me. After half an hour of sitting there, I managed to get myself out of bed. My legs were like jelly. I felt so strange. I knew something had happened to me because I felt like I'd just had rough sex. I could just about make it to the shower without falling and, as I put my knickers on, the panic set in. I went downstairs as fast as my weak legs could take me, but they'd all gone. There was a note on the fridge door that read, 'Hi, Sara, we thought you deserved a lie-in. Don't worry about the agency today, we'll sort everything out. Ring in if you need anything.'

They were being so nice they were starting to scare me. I more or less crawled to the phone and called Timmy. He was the first person who came to mind because he was good with any situation; he always knew what to do. My voice shook with fear as I spoke to him. 'Hello, Timmy, can you help me? I'm scared.'

'What's wrong, babe?' he said, sounding confused. I told him everything that had gone on the night before and the following morning, and he confirmed what I'd been thinking when he said, 'I think you've been raped. Get out of there as fast as you can, ring me when you get back home and I'll pick you up from the station.'

Straight away, I called a taxi. I couldn't pack fast enough. I couldn't wait to get out of there. But I didn't tell my mother, because at the time I believed she would never have forgiven herself if she'd known that she had put me in danger like that again. I also felt I had to protect her, yet I wished I had someone to protect me too.

I never spoke to Timmy again. Even though I knew he would help me, I didn't trust him any more. I still don't know why I called him; it was force of habit, I suppose.

I went straight home and when I got back I couldn't look at Mum, who was constantly asking me why I'd left the agency. Unable to confide in her, I kept on telling myself that she wouldn't have forgiven herself if she'd known what I suspected. I now had to keep yet another secret from her to protect her.

I took the longest of baths, scrubbing every inch of my body until it was red raw. I felt dirty again, just as I had only months before when I used to sleep around. I found myself doing the same things again, like being careful not to touch my vagina with my hands. I thought it was the dirtiest place on earth and would only touch it to wash it, and then only with a sponge. After my bath, I went straight to my room, the only place where I felt safe, no matter what time of day. I tucked myself into my bed where so often I'd slept hour after hour to escape the pain I was suffering.

But my safe little retreat was shattered in a trice when Mum came into my room and said, 'Sara, I've got something to tell you. Your dad has been here. He said he wants to see his kids. I didn't want to tell you while you were away; I thought that I'd worry you. He just turned up out of the blue on the doorstep. He tried to get me to let him see the kids. I asked him to leave us alone and he told me he'd see you all when you're playing outside. He's trying to scare us. I don't know what to do.'

I snapped at her, 'I really don't care, Mum. Fuck him! He's a dirty pervert and he's got a nerve coming here. If I'd been here, I would've killed him. I'm not scared of him any more, even if you are.' I was putting on that brave face again, but the truth was I was very scared, hurt and alone. I was bothered that my father had been there, but right then I couldn't think about it. I could only think about what might have happened to me, and what Timmy had done to me.

I wanted to die, so I grabbed some paracetamol from my drawer and ran and locked myself in the bathroom. Carl must have had some sort of sixth sense, because he started kicking the bathroom door in. I hid in the corner, trying to swallow as many tablets as I could before he got the door open. By the time he burst in, he was too late: I'd taken the lot. He went mad at me, at the same time frantically trying to push his fingers down my throat, but I wouldn't let him. I kept biting him and screaming, 'Leave me to die! Why won't you leave me alone? I can't live like this any more. If there is a God, then I'm being punished for something I did in a previous life, because I don't understand; why else would I be going through all this? Why me? I don't want to be on this hellish place that they call earth any more!'

My poor brother was crying, scared he would lose me. He was on the floor screaming, 'Mum, please help us! Sara has taken an overdose. Mum, help!'

I could hear her running up the stairs. I wanted them to go away, as I knew they could never understand what I was going through. If they had walked in my shoes for a second, they would have done the same thing. I knew that my dad had put them through a lot, but none of them was raped time after time by their own father, and so I believed they could never know how I felt inside. They all thought it was so easy to get over, but nobody was telling me how!

Mum rang an ambulance and then Carl got on the phone to Timmy, threatening to kill him if anything happened to me. They couldn't see that it wasn't all his fault. It wasn't anyone's fault but that bastard of a father of mine. None of it would have happened if he'd been the father he should have been. I would probably never have met half those people and more than likely still have been a virgin.

The ambulance took me to hospital to get my stomach pumped. There, while the doctors were taking care of me, I could hear them asking Mum why she thought I'd taken an overdose. She angered me so much when she whispered, 'She's just split from her boyfriend.'

Going North

The bitch, I thought, if only she could see that it was a combination of everything and the main reason wasn't Timmy. But she was so wrapped up in herself and getting on with her own life that she had neglected to see that I needed help. She was acting like a widow who had been left on the shelf at thirty and needed to be wanted. I hated her. She never understood me, she was too selfish. No one in my family had asked me if I was coping since the day my dad went to prison. In fact, it had been quite the opposite: they expected me to be all right.

My anger got me through having my stomach pumped, and I didn't feel a thing. The doctor let me go home straight away and that night I went clubbing, as I couldn't be around my mum.

Soon I was back to my old ways, going clubbing on my own and sometimes picking up two or three men a week. I was trying to get the hug that I needed from a stranger, because I wasn't getting the love I so longed for at home.

12

A Constant Reminder

Just as I'd been at the hospital many times before that day, so it went on. I was constantly trying to take my own life. Sometimes I meant it, but mostly I was crying out for help. As much as I hate hospitals, I kept on ending up there. My social worker didn't know about this latest overdose. Mum decided that it was best to keep it a secret from him, in case they took me into care. If that were to happen today, they would find out anyway. The system was so different back then: nothing seemed to get done about anything without having to pester them into it.

My trips to the hospital often reminded me of when I had to go in when I was seven. Sometimes when I'd tried to kill myself and an ambulance was called, I used to ask the driver to take me to a different hospital, so that I wouldn't have to think about the way that my father treated me at another time when I was taken in and I needed him. In September of that year, I'd had to go into hospital for an operation. I'd been seeing the doctor for a few months beforehand. Originally, Mum took me because I was throwing up all the time. I ended up telling the doctor that it was because Carl kept on teasing me about my webbed toes; I was born with my two little toes on my right foot joined together. But, even though he did tease me, Carl wasn't the problem at all; he just provided me with an excuse for not telling the doctor the truth: that it was my father's abuse that was making me ill.

I was lying again. I'd been taught to lie by my father, who had drummed lies into my head for so long that it had become second nature to me, even at the age of seven. Mum fell for my excuse too, because she'd heard Carl calling me Duck Foot, Fish Toes, the Webfoot Wonder and all kinds of silly names like that. The names didn't bother me at all, but I needed a stay in hospital; I needed to get away from my father for a while; I needed a break from his abuse, which was getting worse by the day.

Only two nights before I went into hospital to have an operation on my foot – the supposed cause of my troubles – he took me to Nana and Granddad's house and raped me on their front lawn. He knew that they went to bed early and wouldn't see anything. I felt so hurt knowing that the only two people who could have helped me were right there — but totally out of reach. If I'd screamed, he would have beat the living daylights out of me. I kept looking at the window the whole time, hoping that my Granddad would switch on the light and look out. What my dad did that day was his sick way of having a secret dig at my grandfather. He knew that he really disliked him. He also knew that Granddad knew about his physical violence towards my mother.

My father played his many games with my grandparents because he knew that they wouldn't dare to confront him, as they were too afraid that they'd lose their daughter. They certainly weren't stupid, and there's no doubt in my mind that they knew Mum would have stood by him. Taking me there was his only way of getting at Granddad. He wouldn't do anything to his face, he wouldn't have dared; he wasn't a courageous man. Most definitely a total contrast to Granddad, he was weak and pathetic.

When the day arrived for me to go into hospital, I was a little nervous, but in a strange way I was quite looking forward to it. Dad took me there, then Nana came in and took over about an hour after we'd arrived, which meant that Dad could leave. I was so relieved to see the back of him and I stopped worrying about the fact that I didn't have my duvet with me to protect me — only a few starched sheets and a couple of blankets, which didn't make me feel safe at all, at least not until he'd gone.

Nana had snuck in some sweets and she whispered in my ear, 'You've some pineapple rock in the top drawer.

Don't let anyone see them 'cos you'll get me into trouble.' Always up to her tricks, she was a totally defiant person who loved to break the rules.

We had a little giggle, but my smile soon faded when she took me to the playroom and I noticed all the other children, who looked so happy with their mothers and fathers. That was when I started to realise just how bad my life was. Some of them were crying because their parents were leaving. I was baffled, wondering why they were upset. I believed that parents were no good and nanas and granddads were the best, and as I stared at the other children I asked myself, if I'm normal, why do I feel the way I do? Why can't I wait for my dad to leave? He'd always told me that all fathers who loved their children did those things to them, then he told me that I still had to keep our secret, because the fathers who didn't love theirs would never be able to understand that kind of love and would be jealous enough to try to take me away from him. Yet all I could see on the ward were loving fathers and happy children, so I thought, Why aren't I happy? Am I normal? Are they?

Nana had to leave, as we were due to go in for supper. I didn't mind because I was so tired and anxious about my operation, which was scheduled for the following morning, that I wanted to go to bed. Besides, I knew that I was in safe hands there. Anywhere was safer than being at home! I sat on my bed, then Nana came and tucked me in before leaving. As I watched the other children saying goodbye to their mothers and fathers, I started to feel ashamed of myself for hating my dad. I couldn't eat my food, so I turned my back on it all and tried to sleep, but the feelings I had of shame and self-blame kept me wide awake.

I couldn't move, I'd clammed up. I wanted the toilet but I was so scared because I thought that everyone was staring at me because I was so different. I wasn't different at all! But I'd convinced myself otherwise. Because of my fear, I wet myself. I couldn't call out to the nurse because I was so embarrassed. All the things that had happened to me in my tiny life had finally caught up with me. I was in floods of tears, trying very hard to hide them from the nurse who was on her way past. But she noticed, so I lied, telling her that I was sweating. I felt really silly when she noticed that I'd wet myself and told me so. She told me that it was OK to be nervous and not to worry.

After she'd cleaned me up, she patted my head and said goodnight, which made me think about my supposed normal home life even more. If I'd been at home, I would have been given a towel to lie on until the morning, and a beating to go with it.

The following morning, the porters came for me. I was the first person to go down to theatre. Now I wasn't nervous at all. Although there were lots of people surrounding me, all unfamiliar faces, for some reason I felt totally at ease.

They put me to sleep after I'd done the usual count and next thing I knew I was back on the ward with that monster standing over me, staring down at me and smiling with his big yellow teeth. I started to scream for him to get away, then he put his hands over my mouth and made his first demand. 'You'd better shut your fucking mouth before I beat you.'

I wasn't sure if it was a bad dream or maybe the anaesthetic playing tricks with my mind, so I closed my eyes and counted to ten again, hoping that when I opened them he'd be gone. As I opened my eyes, the disappointment was overwhelming: he was still there. I cried out for Nana and, when she and Mum came from behind the curtain, I cried so much that I fell asleep.

When I woke, the monster had gone. And Mum had gone back to work. Then the doctor gave me some bad news. He told Nana that, as long as I walked around that day, I could go home the following afternoon. I tried so hard to limp and skip; you name it, I tried it. I really didn't want to go home. The doctor thought I was scared because of my stitches, so he asked a nurse to help me. I had no choice but to walk and the next day I was sent home as scheduled. Both parents came to pick me up; Mum had taken the day off work. When we arrived home, my dad carried me up the stairs, then said to Mum, 'You cook de dinner and me will bathe her.'

I knew what he was planning but there was nothing I could do. In any case, Mum couldn't have carried me as she was very tiny and I was much too heavy for her to pick up.

Once we were in the bathroom, he locked the door and laid me on the floor, then said, 'I have really missed you, darling.'

As he was taking my clothes off, I knew what he was going to do to me. Then he was on top of me with his big beer belly. I wondered if he was trying to burst my stitches from my skin graft. The doctor had taken skin from my stomach to use on my foot and I had 20 stitches there. He'd told me to be careful not to knock or rub them. But my dad was rubbing them and lying all over them, yet somehow it didn't hurt, because the pain inside my heart was much worse than any physical pain could ever be. I felt trapped and I knew that I wouldn't be going to school for quite a while, which meant that I wouldn't even be able to escape him in that way.

Although I couldn't concentrate there, because I was so worried about what would be waiting for me when I got home, I loved going to school – when he'd let me go. I loved school so much because I could be away from him for a few hours, and most often when my brother and I got back from school he couldn't touch me because we were both there.

I soon realised that my hospital visit wasn't worth it. My plan of a tiny bit of freedom had backfired. I may have had a couple of days away from him, but I would have to spend weeks with him because I couldn't go to school. I couldn't get away from him and I knew that I had plenty more days like those to come. I had no choice because, as he had often reminded me, he owned me. He told me what I could and couldn't do. He had all the power.

Those days have haunted me ever since. Every time I smell a hospital or get a whiff of Dettol, which is what he was putting in my bath that time, I freeze up. I have had to go to the hospital seven times since I stopped harming myself. Fortunately, most of those stays were joyous occasions, but, if I ever had to go there for any other reason than giving birth, or for my children if they were ill, I'd refuse point-blank.

13

Mother's Men

There was the occasional time when I felt that my mother cared for me. After I'd made many attempts to commit suicide, she sat me down and said that she wanted to keep an eye on me. She then offered to start taking me out to clubs and blues parties again. I was so desperate for her attention that I went along with her idea because being out with her, after a few drinks and a dance with her, was the only time I felt loved by her. If I was working (usually either modelling or doing the occasional bit of promotional work for friends) or out with a friend or sexual partner at the time, she'd go out alone. She started going out again to blues parties almost every night of the week, often not coming home until the early hours.

It soon became clear that things were going badly

wrong with Mum's relationship with Terry. Over New Year, she asked me to go to a pub with her for a party and there we bumped into one of Terry's friends. Lance gave me the creeps: he was a very violent and abusive man with no morals whatsoever. He had not long been in the UK, having lived in Jamaica all his life, and often referred to this country as a joke. He had a total disregard for the authorities, calling our police 'pussies' compared with Jamaican police officers. He regularly told us that he would quite happily kill someone without remorse, and believed he would get away with it.

Many times on my nights out, he'd tried to get me to go home with him and we'd had many arguments because of the pressure he used to put on me to leave with him after a blues party. He once asked me to dance with him in a club, but I was probably one of the few people who wasn't fearful of him at all and said, 'Fuck off, old man.'

He laughed in my face and, breathing into my ear, asked, 'Who do you think you is? Lady Di?'

Then Terry stepped in and told me not to mess with him. Almost everyone was scared of Lance, but for some reason his hard exterior didn't faze me at all. He called me 'Lady Di' from that day on. I couldn't stand the man, so as soon as I saw him I promptly left the room and tried to avoid him for the rest of the evening.

That night it wasn't long before a fight broke out: a true cowboy-style brawl, with glasses flying all around the room and people getting barstools thrown at them.

Mother's Men

Everybody who wasn't up for a fight was running and ducking for cover. My mother and I got caught up in the midst of it all and things got so bad that at times I couldn't see her and went into an awful panic. I knew the fight had something to do with Lance; I could feel it in my gut.

After risking everything by standing on a table screaming my mum's name, getting cuts and abrasions from the glass flying around the room, I finally found her. I made a quick decision about the only way I could pull her to safety, and grabbed her by the hair. I got her to crawl with me under the tables and then we managed to get out of the front door.

As we were running, Mum came to a halt and started screaming, 'No, I have to help him.'

I looked round and saw Lance in the middle of the road, stabbing a guy in the stomach. I said to Mum, 'Are you stupid? Come on, we need to get to a payphone and call the police. He doesn't need help. Look at him, he's a monster.'

I had to drag her away to safety because she kept looking back at Lance as he rolled around in the middle of the road with the man that he was fighting.

That was when I saw a glint in her eyes and knew that it was just a matter of time before he was her new man. I was so right: only two weeks later, she threw Terry out of the house while she was drunk, though he'd done nothing to her. I believe she was annoyed at the fact that, no matter how hard she pushed him, he never raised his hand to her. Terry would often laugh things off and had never so much as shouted at her. She used to get so frustrated with his calm and placid nature that she'd scream obscenities in his face, but the most she'd ever get out of him was: 'OK, Rachel, I'll call you tomorrow.' He'd then walk out, leaving her almost foaming at the mouth with anger.

The night that she threw him out, she went out partying by herself and didn't come home. I waited up for her until about three, worried out of my mind that maybe she'd done something stupid because she was upset about the break-up with Terry. I was so fearful for her safety that I cried myself to sleep.

Come the following morning, I woke on the sofa to find her standing over me with a beaming smile on her face. I knew exactly where she'd been and so I was infuriated. A slanging match started and I said to her, 'You've been with Lance, haven't you?' I could have throttled her with my bare hands when she smiled at me and nodded. She did it in a way that suggested I should be happy for her, as though she'd just given me some wonderful news. Either she'd neglected to remember the things I'd told her about him, or the fact that he'd tried to get me to go home with him many times before seemed to give her more reason to want to be with him, as though it was a competition between us. She'd conveniently forgotten how much I hated him and just how much we all loved Terry.

I flew at her in a rage, calling her a dirty slut and a

bad mother. Her response was to ask, 'Why are you so bothered? I know that you and Terry were sleeping together anyway, so you can have him to yourself now, can't you?'

Those words made me sick to my stomach; she disgusted me. I felt so low that I walked out and sat in the park all day. I couldn't believe she thought I would sleep with a man who used to visit my father when I was a child and offer to take me out for the day; a man who used to change my nappy; a man I felt comfortable enough with to call Dad; someone I loved very much indeed.

She'd also failed to see the main reason why I wouldn't want to sleep with her man, which was just that: he was *her* man! I couldn't help thinking that, if she believed that, then what did she think happened between my father and me? Maybe that is why she called me 'Daddy's girl' all the time when I was a child: not because she was happy for me, but because she was jealous of what she thought was our relationship. Her words proved to me, even more than before, that she must have known about my father's sexual abuse of me but hadn't done a thing about it, because she'd treated me in exactly the same way as his girlfriends, which was as a rival, not an abused child. She didn't think that I was an innocent little girl in need of help, but obviously believed that I was to blame too. She'd given me many reasons to leave home and she'd just added another one to my list.

I left home pretty soon after that day, yet I still visited

her regularly, in the hope that she'd want to see me. I'd stay with friends but I kept on going back to her. I was hoping and trying so hard to be her friend, and even after all those years of suffering I believed she still hadn't acknowledged the fact that I needed her to help me. I tried everything to get her to be my mother.

14

Trying to Settle Down

All of that hurt led me to try to find love from a man, a stranger, someone I'd known half an hour, or even five minutes. I would get off with them and afterwards go home and sit in the bath, feeling really dirty before I got into the water but as though nothing had happened when I got out.

Matters had got much worse after things went horribly wrong with Timmy and the modelling agency. My life spiralled downwards very fast. I didn't work for a long while. As well as sleeping with strangers, I was taking drugs and boozing constantly. I knew I was the only person who could stop it, so I decided to settle down with the first single man I met. I believed that settling for anyone who seemed relatively normal was the only way I could stop sleeping around.

I started going to wine bars instead of the trashy dives and blues parties that my mother and father had exposed me to from a very young age. There I hoped to meet someone with a bit more class and be treated a lot better than I had been in the past. I was out clubbing one night on my own when I was approached by an old man who asked me if I could sing. 'Well, I sing in the bath. Does that count?' I asked.

'Yes, if you sing as good as you look, then you'll be fine,' he told me.

I couldn't believe my luck when he handed me his card. I rang him the following day and before I knew it his company was taking me to studios and having talks with a record company. Things went really well and I was enjoying my singing career – until I kept on bumping into Timmy. I couldn't work around him and soon abandoned this new direction, even though they'd built a studio for me close to my mother's house and offered me a contract worth a substantial amount of money. I couldn't be near Timmy. I wasn't that good at singing, although I'm sure I would have made more money than he ever did. But I never had the drive in me to fight against my feelings for him.

Only a few weeks went by before I was deeply regretting my decision to quit singing. Nana came up with an idea for me: glamour modelling. I had no problem with this at all, so I went for it. Within a month, I had worked for a national newspaper and started to earn lots of money. I loved my new career until one day I opened the paper and there I was – nothing unusual in that by now – but when I looked at the date I saw it was my dad's birthday. Then I remembered that the newspaper was his favourite and realised that I'd probably just given him a birthday present that I never wanted him to have. I felt so sick and upset that I told my agent that I wouldn't be working for them as a glamour model ever again.

I went to my old agents but they refused to take me back because they had heard about my work as a glamour model. They said they couldn't have me on their books, as they didn't do porn. They were being very sarcastic, but I suppose I deserved it for going there in the first place. I felt dirty, cheap and totally useless. My idea of finding someone to settle down with was starting to look like my only option.

While out on my new manhunt, I saw one of Timmy's friends, Roger. We were both obviously on the pull. Roger came over to me and offered to buy me a drink, as he'd done so many times before. I'd always told him to fuck off because there was something about his face that I couldn't stand. In any case, I wouldn't have looked at him twice because I was with Timmy at the time. But now I was young, free and single and wanting to settle down, so I thought, Why not?

We talked for a while, mostly about Timmy, and the way he dumped me. Roger said he'd recently been hurt in the same way, then he asked me to meet him for a drink the following weekend so that we could talk some more. He kept on stressing that he believed we had a lot in common and could become very good friends. I knew Roger was single and liked me, so, although I didn't really find him all that attractive, I agreed to meet him, because I truly believed that he could be the one to save me from myself. I was almost 17, with no education, no job and no self-respect. I wanted to settle down as soon as possible, to escape my troubles and finally get some kind of security in my life.

Friends would tell me I was beautiful and talented, but I couldn't see much of a future for myself at all. If I had pursued my modelling career, maybe I would have made a lot of money from it and then I would have had all the security I needed. But, after what happened up North, I couldn't do it any more, because my suspicions about what had happened to me after taking the sleeping pill plagued my mind, and I wouldn't have been able to trust any agent I hadn't met before. After I left, I would work only for people I knew or someone highly recommended by a close friend.

My lack of prospects and mistrust of strangers led me to the conclusion that a solid, long-lasting relationship was my only way forward. So I went along for that drink with Roger and we talked some more about Timmy and our past. He then invited me back to his flat after assuring me that he wouldn't try to sleep with me or anything at all. I was so pleased to meet a gentleman, and the fact that he'd invited me back to his place proved to me that he wasn't living with anyone. Even though I'd heard that Roger was single, I was still very wary of any man who said that he was, especially after what Timmy did to me. So I was pleasantly surprised to discover that Roger was definitely single.

We started dating and within three months I moved into his flat. It was like a dream come true to me. He was taking care of me and everything to do with the flat. I didn't want for anything, but I wanted to start paying my way, so I went looking for work. Walking into the local pub, I thought, Well, pulling pints can't be that hard. Although I was only 16, I told the owner that I was 18 and asked him for a job. Luckily for me, he was a sucker for a pretty face and, although he wasn't desperate for any staff, he took me on. He was also a good friend of my friends Andrew and Lisa, so I suggested he ring them for a reference. They told him that I was a hard worker, so thanks to them I got the job.

Roger would sit in the bar most nights after he had finished work. He wasn't a big drinker, but he liked the company of the regulars; most of them worked in the local theatre and they were loads of fun to be around. Although working in the pub turned out to be much harder than I'd predicted, I really loved it and it was much better than any modelling job I'd ever had. My boss, Pete, and I became very close friends. I even started calling him Dad and, although it was a bit of an ongoing joke, deep down I meant it. Pete was someone I could look up to. I told him everything and he was very understanding, always giving me good advice and lots of much-needed hugs.

Although Roger and I had only been together for three months, I decided that the time was right to propose to him. I had spoken to Pete about my plans and he knew me well enough to not try to change my mind. He knew that once I got an idea in my head the easiest option would be to go along with it, so, slightly hesitantly, he went along with my intention to marry Roger. Pete and I planned a surprise for him. Pete cooked a meal and laid out a beautiful table in the pub. We planned it for a Sunday evening because that time was usually quiet, whereas Sunday lunchtime was very busy.

I called Roger and asked him to pick me up for nine. Pete had left me in charge of the pub for the rest of the evening. Roger walked in and his face lit up when he saw the table. I could tell by his face that he knew what my plans were. Before I could say a word, he held me tight and said, 'Yes I will.' That made me so happy. I'd been very nervous about asking Roger to marry me and he'd just made it a whole lot easier.

From that day, things moved on very fast. Within days, we were making plans for our wedding. I had never been so happy, and for the first time in years I felt safe and secure. Meeting Roger was like a godsend after my long and arduous journey. Strangely enough, I believed he was

my saviour and for quite a while I truly believed that my
journey prior to meeting him had ended and I was on a
new road to wonderful happy bliss, hopefully with plenty
of peace and love. I had no idea that I had so much
further to go.

But deep down I knew I could only rely on myself.
After all, self-sufficiency was something that I'd learned
from a young age — well, since I could reach the food
cupboards anyway. But by now I had somehow managed
to disconnect myself from reality and had suddenly taken
on a 'little princess' mentality. I often slipped into my
imaginary life where nothing painful or frightening was
happening and everything was perfect. This was the way
that I'd learned to protect myself, my barrier against the
confusion on the outside.

My mother was very disappointed when I announced
my wedding plans. In truth, she was furious, begging me
not to go through with it, and even tried to get Lance to
give a big speech to Roger on a night out with them. He
tried a heavy-handed approach, coming across all fatherly
to Roger. Which was a bit ironic considering Roger was
older than he was. He was questioning him in such a way
that if Roger didn't know any different he'd have believed
that Lance was my dad.

I made sure that Roger took no notice of what Lance
had to say, and forced my mother to come round to the
idea of us getting married. It was my cunning plan, as I
needed her to sign the papers, and I begged and pleaded

with her. By taking the spoiled-child approach, I believed I'd make her give in to my demands; she always did, because it was easier than saying no after being bombarded hundreds of times with 'Please, Mum, I'm begging you'. I used the fact that I'd behaved in such a terrible way in the past and now needed to settle down. I also asked her what was so wrong with people getting married at a young age, because she'd done it too.

Eventually, she gave in and came with me to the registry office to arrange everything. She also went along with the wedding, but on one condition. She told me that I wasn't allowed to invite Terry and, if I did, she wouldn't come. She knew I wanted him to come and she also knew he'd done nothing to warrant her saying that he couldn't. But no amount of talking would change her mind: she was out to please her new man and nothing else mattered. I felt confused and angry at the time because, although I wanted Granddad to give me away, I also felt that somehow Terry had a right to do so too. After all, he had been a good father substitute for me and I loved him. I loved him like I'd loved no other man, apart from Granddad. I had to try to keep the peace by assuring my mother that I wouldn't invite him. Deep down I was hurting and needed him there, so I went to see him, and arranged for him to hide at the back of the church.

Terry also came to the reception, but he stayed outside, hiding around the corner of the pub, and had a drink with me to celebrate. Then he gave me his best wishes and left before my mother saw him. That truly hurt. He should have been able to give a speech and dance with me, just like a father would. My mother's wishes ruined what was supposed to be the best day of my life.

Roger and I had married within seven months of meeting. We had our first child, Jasmine, a year later, which was when I started to feel like a real adult, even though things weren't as perfect as they seemed. I was trying so hard to keep up appearances and have my little fairy-tale marriage look perfect to the outside world.

I visited my mother at least four times most weeks, trying everything to get her to love Jasmine more than she had apparently loved me. Most times, as soon as I walked through the door I'd place Jasmine in her arms and say, 'Go to Nana, darling.' I was hoping and praying that my mother felt something more for her than she did for me. I wanted to know that she was human, with real feelings. Because I craved her love, I decided that, if she couldn't give it to me, then, because I loved Jasmine so much, getting some sort of love through my daughter was enough.

That period was a very strange one for me. Part of me resented my mother and part of me was still seeking her approval for everything that I did. During my visits, she wanted for nothing. I wouldn't let her lift a finger: I did all her housework for her and I wouldn't miss a thing. I'd pull out the sofas, beds, bread bin and everything: all the usual spring-cleaning jobs. I'd do the housework for her three or four times a week without receiving any thanks and quite often not even a smile. She was so ungrateful that even ignorant Lance noticed and would say how well I'd done the work and make a point of telling her that she had a wonderful caring daughter. His words went in one ear and out of the other. I often wondered if she had anything between her ears. I should have known at the time that the only thing that my mother ever cared about was having something between her legs!

I was so used to her cold response that if ever she did say or do anything nice I'd freeze up in an instant. I wasn't used to her being nice and, although that was all that I'd been wishing for, I often thought that she was up to or after something. So her kindness had the opposite effect and left me feeling icy. After all, she often asked me for money – after she'd smiled in my face.

So there I was just struggling through unusual difficulties and creating this world that wasn't there, keeping up the pretence that everything was perfect. The only thing that got me through the toughest times was my gut feelings. I would agonise: is she being nice to me because she wants some money? Or has she finally realised that she loves me? I mostly went with my gut instinct and didn't mistake her kindness for weakness. She hadn't come round to the idea that we could be close and love each other, she just wanted something, or she was only smiling because Lance or someone else that she wanted to make herself look normal to was there at the time.

Trying to Settle Down

Being so desperate to have a mother, I would give her money all the time, which, along with many other things, was causing problems in my home. Roger was always telling me, 'Cut her off. She doesn't deserve you, she's a cold-hearted cow.' This made me even more determined to keep speaking to her. I believed the reason Roger was saying that was because our marriage was going bad and he wanted to keep me all to himself. I thought that he was so manipulative and wanted to grind me down so much that I only had him to fall back on and then he could sleep around and treat me as badly as he liked and I'd have nobody to turn to.

My mother wasn't there for me to turn to, but at the time I convinced myself that she was. In any case, I was so wrapped up in trying to get her to love me that I found it impossible to let go. I was more focused on what I could do next to grab her attention than on letting go so that I could start to heal my wounds. At the time, I felt as though I was in a lengthy war and was the only soldier in a gigantic battlefield, with no weapons to fight back at the world with. I felt left with a wound that could never heal because it kept on getting gashed open by all around me. By then, even my husband, who had promised to love and honour me for the rest of my days, was fighting me, leaving me hurt, angry and very alone.

I'd call my mother many times, crying, asking her opinion on Roger's games. She would always tell me that I was being paranoid and should learn to trust him. It's ironic, because she hated Roger right up until the point that he started cheating and hitting me, but as soon as he started to treat me badly she began to announce to anyone who'd listen to her that there was nothing wrong with him and I was being silly, paranoid and totally neurotic. I found myself starting to mimic my mother at that point in time, by having child after child in the hope that my marriage to Roger would somehow miraculously become something like my grandparents'. A happy marriage, with no serious problems and no outside influences to destroy us.

But my plan wasn't succeeding and I blamed Roger for cheating on me, believing that it was all his fault. But it wasn't all down to him. I was also bringing other people into our marriage by letting my mother come between us, often spending valuable time with her, trying to get her to see that I needed her to love me, when I should have been at home with my husband talking through our problems. I believe now that, if I had stayed at home and concentrated on my marriage, instead of giving so much time to my mother and so little to being his wife, maybe I would have seen him for what he was a lot sooner. Then, either we wouldn't have lasted so long or we would have worked things out. And he wouldn't have cheated on me, because we would have been too strong for him to want to do so, and I definitely wouldn't have suffered inside, feeling lonely, for as long as I did.

I resented Roger because he'd broken my trust in him

by cheating on me. I'd often stressed to him that if he did that he would ruin everything, because there was no way that I was going to live my life the same way as my mother did. No way was I going to allow my husband to sleep with other women and hurt me in that way. Or let him drive me to the point where I felt the need to compete with them, just like my mother had, by having a child whenever they were pregnant too, or just cooking lots of meals for him in the hope that he would come home and dine with me instead of them, and hoping and praying that my cooking tasted better than theirs.

What I couldn't see was that I *was* being my mother. I was allowing him to get away with cheating on me, because I was so weak that I just wanted someone to love me, no matter what pain came with that love.

15

Betrayed

I knew not long after our first child, Jasmine, was born that our marriage wouldn't last, but, despite the fact that I had caught him out in many lies, I kept on working at it. The first time he cheated was just after Jasmine arrived. He'd gone away to work for six weeks and came back with six women's telephone numbers. Six weeks, six numbers: he definitely didn't waste any time while he was away.

It all seemed to happen so fast too. One minute we were sitting on our bed a few days after Jasmine was born, worrying about the fact that he would be going off in a few days' time. The next thing we knew the day had arrived for him to leave. I remember sitting on the bed holding Jasmine, watching him pack, then bursting into tears and not being able to stop. I never told him, but I was so scared at the thought of being left alone to cope with my first child. The only thing that got me through it was the fact that I'd practically raised all my mother's kids by myself, so I knew what I was doing when it came to the basics. But, despite all that knowledge, I still wanted Roger there with us, because I had paranoid thoughts about something going wrong with our daughter.

As the days went by, I started to feel more at ease with the situation. Roger called us every night to talk about Jasmine's progress. I'd give him a quick call whenever she woke up for her nightly feed, so that he could say goodnight to her. That changed to one phone call per day again when Jasmine started sleeping through the night at only three weeks old. She was a greedy little so-and-so by that point and obviously didn't need a feed during the night because she would guzzle so much milk during the day.

One night Roger didn't ring, so I gave him a quick call so that he could say goodnight to Jasmine, but when I got through to his room a woman answered the phone. I said hello and a woman sighed gently and put the phone down straight away. I couldn't believe what I had just heard, so I rang back straight away but there was no answer. This had never happened before, so I started to wonder if he was cheating on me. In a desperate panic, I rang the front desk of the hotel and, when they told me that Roger was definitely in his room and I'd called the right room, as far as I was concerned it had been confirmed. I'd caught

Roger cheating on me but there was nothing I could do to prove it. I knew he would deny everything by saying that there must have been a mix-up with the rooms. I also knew that he was probably with another woman while I was lying awake worrying myself sick, wondering how I'd ever forgive him.

I thought about what he could have been doing all night. The following morning, I picked up the phone to call him but stopped myself, knowing that I had to concentrate on Jasmine. I definitely didn't want to be consumed by the rage I was feeling. I knew that, if I called him and he denied it, I would throw a fit, and I didn't want my baby to see me upset. I'd seen enough of that kind of behaviour when I was a young child. I knew how it felt to witness your parents fighting and arguing. I definitely didn't want that for my daughter, so I stopped myself from making a big mistake, because my plan was to never let my kids see me upset, no matter what age they were.

Our phone calls stopped. I didn't want to call him in case another woman answered again. I just didn't want to know if he was cheating. I couldn't face it, because there were so many weeks to go before he came home that I would have been putting myself through hell if I'd kept on ringing him. I wanted to wait until he came home to confront him, so that I could see his reaction face to face. It felt as though my whole world was falling apart and that everything was out of my hands, but because he was so far away from me I had no choice but to wait.

The days seemed to go by very slowly, and it wasn't long before severe depression set in and got the better of me. I don't know whether I had post-natal depression or if my feelings were due to the fear of Roger possibly sleeping around, but my anxiety got worse by the day. I was sleeping all the time and hardly ever leaving the flat. I was supposed to start back at work in the pub four weeks after Jasmine was born, but I couldn't do it. I rang Pete to tell him that I was too ill. I couldn't face other people. I believed that if they knew something was wrong they would all be talking about us behind our backs, saying how they'd known it wouldn't last, so I thought it best to stay away. I lay in bed most of the time, clutching my duvet, praying for my marriage to last longer than the five minutes that most people had probably predicted, and hoping that I was wrong about Roger.

Mum and Carl noticed that I was depressed. They took it upon themselves to call Roger at work and he came home a week early. When he saw me, he called the doctor out straight away. I was given anti-depressants, which I took for a while, but they made me feel worse because I knew that there was a reason for my depression. I wasn't just depressed; I had a good reason to be down in the dumps. I believed that my husband had slept with another woman and in my eyes that's enough reason to be down. I also knew that the only way to solve my problem was to confront him. I chose my moment and went in for the kill. I'd held it in for long enough, fearful of his reaction and of finding out the truth, but now I'd had enough of not knowing.

While he was out, I cooked a meal, and when he walked in he had a confused look on his face. 'Wow, are you cooking? Those tablets must be working.'

This comment had already angered me, so I turned to him and said, 'No, actually we need to fucking talk.' I threw the dinner on the floor, screaming at him, 'I've had enough of this. Have you cheated on me?'

I knew he had, because his face was riddled with guilt when he said, 'No, don't be silly.'

By then, I was past boiling point, shouting, 'You liar, you fucking liar. I got through to your room. Your trollop answered the phone, I heard her. Stop lying.'

He started yelling back, which again spelled guilt to me. 'You're crazy, you could have got through to any room. What is wrong with you? You're mad, you have post-natal depression, you need help, you're paranoid.'

Suddenly, he had become totally unsupportive and was obviously manipulating the situation by bringing up post-natal depression. Roger was guilty, though I had no proof. But his reaction only made me stronger, more determined to finish my course of tablets and get better. I realised that he was willing to make me feel as though I was going mad to escape the truth. That really angered me, because I know when someone is lying to me. I grew up around lies and I can spot one a mile off.

I walked out, taking Jasmine with me. I needed time to

think. I came to the conclusion that, because of my age, he thought he could manipulate me, make me think that I was just a paranoid little girl. But he had neglected to see that I may not have had much to do with books like he had, and I may not have had any qualifications, but I had a degree or two in life, and even at the age of 18 I'd certainly seen an awful lot. I knew a manipulative bastard when I saw one and I wasn't willing to let anyone talk down to me because I was younger than them. The way I saw it, if he thought I was a kid, he shouldn't have agreed to marry me and, if he didn't believe I was just a kid, he shouldn't have been trying to talk to me as though I was. I knew it was best that I left for a while. I gave myself some time to think about it all and plan how to approach the matter again.

A couple of weeks later, I was still wound up about it, so I went back to the flat while he was at work and went through his things. When I found six women's names and numbers in his tour bag, my fears were confirmed. I knew then that I'd been right to leave him. He was a cheating, manipulative liar – he'd even folded the numbers tightly and placed them in a small barely noticeable compartment. That was when it became obvious that he was a liar, but what made it worse was the amount of numbers I'd found.

I was beginning to wish I hadn't looked when the phone rang. It was my mum. I burst into floods of tears and told her what he'd done. She suggested I wait for him to get back and talk to him. I don't know why I told her anything – she was the last person who'd know what to do. She'd let men walk all over her all her life and the fact that they cheated was an accepted part of life for her. It was obvious she would tell me to talk to him and work things out, because that's exactly what she'd done many times in her life.

As I sat and waited for him to come home, I could feel all the resentment and hate for him brewing up inside me, thinking to myself the whole time that if I was brave enough I'd probably attack him. Those hours seemed like days and by the time he arrived home I'd wound myself up into a frenzy. As soon as he walked through the door, I turned to him and screamed, 'Get out! I hate you. How could you try to make me think I was mad when it was you all along?'

He refused to leave, insisting that it was all in my head. 'Sara, I'm keeping the numbers for my friend at work. His wife checks all his stuff as soon as he walks into his house. He's been caught cheating so many times. He's a bloody sex addict. His wife doesn't understand, so he's asked me to look after them for him.'

Back then, I thought I knew all the tricks in the book, but in truth I was very naive! Although most times I'd protest at first, I often fell for Roger's games. What he'd said about his colleague had thrown me. I knew about the man's compulsive adultery and, although I knew that what Roger was saying was outrageous, I thought about his friend and the things I knew about that he'd done, and I started to find what Roger was saying very believable. I was very confused, but I had no choice but to give him the benefit of the doubt.

Nevertheless, those phone numbers played on my mind for weeks, so I planned a night out for the two of us. I left Jasmine at Mum's for the night and arranged to meet Roger after work. I had booked a restaurant and as we got comfortable over our meal I started off the conversation by reminiscing about our whirlwind romance and how much I wanted us to work things out. But I knew I had to take another approach to asking him about the other women that he'd possibly cheated with, so I said, 'Roger I grew up with lies. I don't want the same for us. It's not healthy for you, myself and Jasmine to have this hanging over our heads. If you tell me the truth now, I will forgive you, we can have some counselling and work at our marriage, but, if I find out at a later date that you are lying, I will divorce you straight away.'

I was lying but I desperately wanted to know the truth. I needed to find out if my husband was a lying, manipulative monster, just like my father. I had planned to divorce him if he confessed to sleeping with anyone else, not because he'd done it but because he had lied to me and made me feel as though I was going crazy. I knew that Roger couldn't handle his booze, so while we were talking I kept topping up his glass with wine and telling him, 'We can work things through, I promise. Just tell me the truth.'

Betrayed

He thought he was the only person who could be manipulative in our relationship, but I proved him wrong. He felt so stupid when he confessed all and I stood up and smacked him in the mouth and then walked out. He quickly came running after me, doing his usual grovelling. 'Sara, you wouldn't drop it. I thought it would shut you up.'

I couldn't be around him any longer, so I raced home to pack a few things, then left to stay at my mum's. Although I hated being there, it was better than staying at home with him and torturing myself. Besides, once I was at her house she never questioned me at all. I used to wish that she would, but she stayed out of my business – unbelievable, considering that she was constantly in it when I was at home with Roger. I suppose that my going to stay with her had made her eat a bit of humble pie, given the number of times she'd stressed that I didn't have the bottle to leave him.

The following day I made an appointment with a solicitor to start divorce proceedings. I didn't want a divorce, but I felt that our marriage had gone past the point of no return.

Just a few days later I was rushed into hospital with abdominal pains. The doctor checked me over, then told me I was pregnant and possibly having a miscarriage. I was absolutely devastated. Straight away, Mum rang Roger and he raced over to see me. Because of the unplanned pregnancy, I felt that we had to discuss our issues of trust, and maybe think about going to Relate and working things out.

After two days, I went back home with Roger to get some rest. The thought of being a single mother with two kids worried me immensely and I didn't think I'd cope at all. So I decided to try my hardest to put everything that had happened behind us. For a while, things worked out, but I couldn't forget what he had put me through. We started arguing a lot, and after a short time it turned into violence. Out of frustration, he was lashing out every time I brought up the affairs. I soon became very scared of him, which resulted in my going back to see my solicitor at least once a week, although nothing came of it for a while because the fear of being alone was too much for me.

Despite many problems in my pregnancy, which I now put down to the stress that Roger was putting me through, my second child, Toni, came along safely. I decided that life with him was definitely not the same any more. We'd been through enough together and it had left me feeling at the end of my tether. Finally, I found the courage to do something about the mess that I'd found myself in, and told the local housing department about my violent relationship with Roger. Without hesitation, they put me in a women's hostel. It wasn't very nice there, but they had guaranteed that within weeks they would offer me a house.

16

A Fresh Start

That October, the offer of a house materialised. Although it was in the same town, I felt happy that it was far enough away from Roger for me to start a new life with the children. But the guilt of keeping his children away from him was all too much for me to deal with. I knew that eventually I would give in to my emotions and call him, because I'd had to face the fact that I didn't have a father in my life and I didn't want the same for my girls. So I bit the bullet and called Roger.

It all started off fine. The visits we arranged for him to be with the children gave me a break, which left me time on my hands to decorate my new house. He kept on telling me how sorry he was every time he dropped the kids home. Eventually, he started sending me flowers every day. His overtures soon worked and, although I had mixed emotions about taking him back, I tried hard to make things work again. I often thought about my mother and the amount of times she'd accepted from her partners the kinds of things that Roger was doing to me. I felt ashamed of myself at times, and because of that I didn't want to end up living my life in her shadow, accepting whatever life threw at me, just to have a peaceful life, just so I wouldn't get a beating or have to deal with my partner cheating on me.

But there was no longer any trust between us. I tried very hard to get it back but it was too late. He'd ruined everything by cheating just after I'd given birth to our first child and, even though he tried very hard to win back the trust, I resented him too much by then.

It wasn't long before my suspicions were confirmed. Roger had cheated again only six months into our attempt to save our marriage. I felt weak and had given up. I didn't even have the energy left to confront him. I found myself doing exactly what my mother used to do, and got pregnant again. I stupidly thought that having another child would save our marriage. We were constantly splitting up and getting back together, which suited Roger, because while we were apart he got the chance to spend time with his mistress. I let things slide and got on with my pregnancy.

When I had only two months to go, Mum rang me out of the blue. She was very upset and shouted at me, 'Why didn't you tell me?'

A Fresh Start

'Tell you what?' I said.

'It's all over the papers. That agency up North have been caught.'

'Caught doing what?'

'Leon and his friend have been arrested for rape and sexual assault on a lot of the models. They allege the girls have been drugged.'

I was in a state of shock, with all my fears and suspicions about what might have happened to me reawakened. I felt guilty for not telling Mum about it, but at the time I thought I was making the right decision. After that phone call, I became very depressed. My nightmare had begun again: not only was Roger cheating on me again, but also my suspicions of being raped while drugged were plaguing me. Not only that, but I'd upset my mother, who would never understand why I couldn't have told her at the time. Part of me wondered why she was so upset about not knowing, because she would have done nothing to help me at the time. Besides, she would have been more upset for herself than for me.

I was so down in the dumps that I decided to see a doctor and ask for some counselling. At the age of 22, I had started to feel intense pain about all the things that I had endured. I told myself, I have children now, I can't just hide under my duvet any more and hope that it will all go away. I knew that I had to be strong for my children. My counselling sessions went really well. I found myself getting stronger and stronger every week. I realised that all my life I'd been so worried about other people's feelings that I'd neglected to think of myself. So that is what I started to do.

I tried to discover if there was any evidence to prove my suspicions that I had been drugged and then raped while working for the modelling agency up North, but failed to make any progress.

I got fed up with not getting help with my problems but I decided I was a whiner and tried to put the past behind me and get some control back in my life. That was when I went to a newspaper and sold my story for £3,000. I used the money to take driving lessons and buy a car. Learning how to drive with a big bump in front of me wasn't as easy as I thought it would be. I was so stressed with the driving test coming up, and the fact that I was doing an intensive course was making me ill. The result was that I went into early labour. I was very silly to do so much while I was pregnant, and my stupidity resulted in me missing my driving test. Fortunately, my little 5lb 13oz baby girl, Beth, was so healthy that I took her home the same day.

My driving instructor had managed to get me another slot for my test the following day. Although I'd only just given birth, there was no stopping me! I was determined to get on with my life and take back some control of the horrible situation that I was in. After I passed my test, my life started to change dramatically.

I knew it was only a matter of time before I was a single

mother, so that is how I started to act. I stopped including Roger in everything I did with the children. I became a very independent women and a proud mother. I felt especially close to Beth because I'd been through some major life changes while I was pregnant with her. It felt as though she'd been there with me every step of the way. In my mind, she knew me more than anyone else could, and because of that we had a special bond that could never be broken.

I can safely say now that it was at 22 that I first felt like a woman and called myself one instead of referring to myself as 'a girl'. I was getting mentally stronger by the day and I knew it wouldn't be long before I could go it alone.

17

Walking Away

Meanwhile, things remained pretty much the same until at last I found the strength to walk away from my marriage. By that time, I had learned not to talk to my mother about how I was feeling, because before I decided to leave Roger I'd often threatened to and she had repeatedly told me that I wouldn't. She would laugh at me and tell me I was being really silly to even contemplate going through with it. Many times, she told me to stop lying and asked me if I was having my period or just a bad day. That left me feeling stupid and totally lacking in confidence.

For a time, I believed her words and failed to carry out my threat to leave. But what I hadn't seen at the time was that she didn't want me to leave him for cheating on me, since she hadn't left my father when he did the same. She wanted me to live pretty much the same life as she had, and was still living. I suppose it made her feel that she wasn't the only weak woman on the planet who would accept that kind of behaviour from her partner.

Oddly, she often acted as though she wanted us all to grow up and be just like her and my father, but in reality she never did show us a better way of life. There were many times in the past when I heard her telling Carl that he was just like my father. I never understood why she would want to liken her son to that monster but, as I've said before, there are many issues to do with my mother's behaviour that I still don't get to this day.

When I finally found the courage to get a divorce, I waited a while until I was one hundred per cent certain about asking my husband to leave and then I told my mother that I'd done it. She wasn't very happy about it and constantly asked if I'd consider having Roger back, but I stood my ground because by that stage I knew that my marriage was definitely over.

It wasn't long before I started dating Tyrone. He was a young man I'd met in our local wine bar while I was having a chat with a girlfriend and some much-needed Dutch courage on the day that I decided to ask Roger to leave. Tyrone was another partner that my mother didn't approve of. He and I met through my friend Linda. I'd known Linda most of my life but hadn't seen her for years. Then I bumped into her on a night out with Carl and things progressed from there. I needed someone to talk to and I knew that Carl would be the only person to listen to me without saying that he'd told me so or giving me some speech about how marriage shouldn't be taken too lightly. We met at our local pub and talked for a while about my failing marriage, throwing in all the usual 'should haves', 'could haves' and 'would haves'. Then he let out a big sigh and told me he was relieved that I'd come to that decision and offered me his full support, which truly meant a lot to me at the time. Especially as I'd never had support from anyone before.

We had a real laugh that day and I was so relieved to get the whole thing off my chest that I got terribly drunk. Just as we were daring each other to go up for the karaoke, a very low female voice came from behind us. 'Hello, Sara. Hello, Carl.'

'Who is she?' said Carl.

'I don't know,' I answered, shrugging.

The woman rushed up and hugged us. 'Don't you remember me? I'm an old friend of the family. We used to babysit you sometimes when you were kids. It's Linda, don't you remember me?'

I couldn't remember her face but the name rang a bell. As we all got talking, Linda brought up what my father did to me. She was very angry and assured me that she had nothing more to do with his family.

Linda and I got on very well as we had many things in common, and we became very close friends. She had been through a lot too and knew what I meant when I said that I felt like a single mother, even though I was married. I felt alone, but at the same time that was what I had planned for the near future and I couldn't wait!

The day I met Tyrone, Linda and I were having a chat about men and how they all think they're God's gift, when she started telling me about this guy that she'd seen on the bus. She went on about him for quite a while, telling me just how much he looked like her son. I just humoured her because, although her son was good-looking, I thought that he was so different to most guys I'd ever seen that there couldn't be anyone who looked that much like him. But she went on and on. 'He looks just like my son. I heard about him years ago, they went to the same school, but, although they look alike, he is so much more polite than my son. There he is! How strange, he's just walked in!'

I thought, What are the chances of that happening?

I didn't think he looked like her son at all, so I told her so, but she started up again. She's so much like me: once she has an idea in her head, she really sticks with it. I suppose that was why I liked her so much. Anyway, she kept insisting, 'He does look like him. Look at him, he's the spitting image of him.' We agreed to disagree. But then she embarrassed us all by calling him over. 'Tyrone, come here. How are you?' I cringed because I knew she would probably embarrass him too. She introduced us. 'Sara, this is Tyrone. Tyrone, this is Sara. We were just talking about you. I can't believe you walked in. I'd only just said your name.' She was terrible, she never shut up, but she was very funny and I loved her.

Tyrone didn't know where to look, and he seemed to whisper as he said, 'Would you like a drink?'

Linda replied, 'No thank you, we've just paid for our drinks, but I'll let you get the next round in.' I could have slapped her. 'Calm down, Sara,' she said. 'I'm only having a laugh. Tyrone, come and sit with us, and bring your friend too.'

I hadn't even noticed his friend. I was too busy staring at Tyrone to see if I could spot the resemblance to Linda's son. Tyrone then introduced us to Dean. As usual, Linda started up the conversation, telling Tyrone again how she'd just been telling us that he looked so much like her son.

Tyrone frowned, sighed and said, 'Yes, Linda, I've heard of him. A lot of my old school friends used to tell me that I had a twin. I've never met him but I'm sure he's gorgeous.'

Everyone was laughing. He was a funny guy and, despite his earlier embarrassment, very confident too. I liked that and we were getting on really well.

When Dean noticed my wedding ring and asked if I was married, Linda couldn't resist the cue. 'Not for long,' she said. 'As soon as she's finished her pint she's going home to sling him out.'

Although shocked that Linda could be so cruel, all I

could do was laugh. The way it came out it sounded so funny, but deep down I was a bag of nerves. I was dreading the fact that I had to go home to talk to Roger, but I had no intention of changing my mind, although I was certain it would be the hardest thing I'd ever done.

Tyrone and I were getting on so well that I decided to stay a while longer. Just one more drink, I kept telling myself. We were joking about Dean's lecherous behaviour as he walked around the pub flirting with any female that he could. I normally find men like him annoying, but somehow I found Dean's way of chatting up the girls very amusing. He was clumsy and not the type of guy many women would take very seriously, but Tyrone, so cool, was a total contrast to his best friend.

I liked him and he liked me, it was so obvious. As Linda had already told him and Dean about my marital problems, he became increasingly concerned and asked me if I would be OK when I got home. He seemed genuinely concerned for me as he could see that I was worrying myself sick about it all. Giving me his number, he said, 'Ring me at any time if you need someone to talk to.'

I took it but then felt guilty because I hadn't spoken to Roger about the divorce yet and already I'd pulled. My guilt was terrible because I really liked Tyrone, yet I knew that to get involved with someone at this point would be very wrong. I went to the ladies' to throw his number away, thinking to myself, He'll never know a thing. Anyhow, I'll probably never see him again, so it doesn't matter. Apart from the guilt, I didn't need a new relationship right then, not with all that was going on in my life already.

I shook myself and reminded myself why I was there. It was to talk about my marriage ending. Yet, as soon as I'd thrown away the number, I sat there with Tyrone and quickly regretted it. Talking to him felt so right that I didn't want it to end. When those thoughts entered my mind, I knew that it was time to leave. 'Goodbye, everyone,' I said. 'I have to go home to sort this mess out.'

Tyrone looked disappointed and said, 'Have one more drink with me. I'd like to get to know you a little better.'

He was very persistent and seemed like the type of person who would be willing to do anything to get what he wants. I accepted his offer and we talked for a while longer, but it wasn't long before the panic started to set in. The longer I stayed there, the more worried I got about going home to face Roger. Tyrone noticed a change in my personality and grabbed my hand and said I would be fine. At that moment, I realised that I could feel something real for him, something special, without my past affecting my judgement. I wasn't looking for a father figure, I wasn't looking for someone to save me from myself. I just wanted him, without having any other reasons for getting into a relationship.

It felt good, but scary. Just knowing that I'd thought many times in the past that I was in love only to find out that I wasn't put me off having anything to do with

Tyrone. I didn't want to hurt him, but the more we talked, the more I knew my feelings were true. It's funny how love comes to you when you least expect it, at times when you think you really don't need it. Because of my confused state of mind, I decided to leave. Tyrone stood up and tried everything to spend just a little more time with me. He even pulled the 'Which way are you going?' stunt. I started to tell him and quickly wished I'd never opened my mouth when he said, 'I'm going that way, would you drop us off?'

I would have made some excuse but Linda said, 'Go on, it's only around the corner from your house.'

If only the ground could swallow me up, I thought. Please do it now. Feeling as though I'd been left with no choice, I agreed to drop them home.

We were on our way when Tyrone noticed that he'd left his bag in the pub and, silly me, I offered to take them back to get it. 'Tyrone, I will take you back, but I have to check on the kids first.'

Back at the house, I invited Tyrone and Dean in. They were worried that Roger might not appreciate two strange young lads being with his wife, but I told them that I would tell him that they were friends of Linda's. In any case, Roger wasn't the jealous type. I introduced them to him, then they waited for me in the living room. I could see that Tyrone felt very uncomfortable being around Roger; he looked angry and I think he was jealous in his own little way.

I gave the kids a kiss and asked Roger if he would put

them to bed early because I wanted us to talk when I got back from taking Tyrone and Dean home. He must have had a sense of what I wanted to talk about, because he was doing his usual trick of pretending not to hear me, in the hope that I'd forget and not mention it again. I had a feeling that he would keep the kids up as long as possible, so that we wouldn't be able to talk when I got back, but I knew that the kids wouldn't be able to stay up past nine, so I stayed out as long as possible, knowing that they'd be asleep by that time, of their own accord.

When we arrived outside Tyrone's house, Dean got out of the car. I panicked a bit, wondering what Tyrone was going to say, then he said, 'Sara, will you ring me?'

That was when I had to tell him the truth. 'Tyrone, I threw your number away. I'm too nervous to get involved with anyone else, especially after my bad joke of a marriage.'

'You don't have to get involved,' he said. 'I'll write my number out for you again. I want you to keep it and, if ever you need a friend, call me. There doesn't need to be any strings attached.'

I couldn't believe how sensible and kind he was. He was only 18 and I was 23, but he had more sense than I did. When he grabbed my hand, I tried fighting it, but I really liked him. I knew also that he'd be an easy person to love. My luck was so bad and even more typical was the fact that I'd met the man of my dreams in the midst of all the mess that I was in. To be left with no choice but to walk away was killing me inside. I just wanted to kiss him. I certainly didn't want to drive away, but I had to, so I said goodbye, then drove away with what felt, at the time, like a broken heart.

I sat outside my house for hours, not wanting to go inside and tell Roger that our marriage was over. I was feeling guilty because of how I already felt about Tyrone, but I told myself not to accept any blame, because it wasn't me who ruined our marriage. Eventually, I dragged myself inside but couldn't find the courage to tell him. I went up to bed and tossed and turned for hours before I got up and went back downstairs. 'Roger, I'm ready to talk,' I told him.

He gulped and said, 'OK, Sara, but can you sit down first? You're making me nervous.'

Then, because of my own nerves and anger, it all came out wrong. 'You should be. Now why don't you leave this house? You've ruined our marriage. I hate you and I don't want to be married to you a minute longer.'

It was the worst possible way I could have dealt with the situation, but I'd got the job done. I'd never been able to talk to Roger. He was 13 years older than me and often made me feel like a kid, so I found it hard to express myself to him. But I had no excuse for saying what I'd said to him. I'd just blamed him for absolutely everything and it wasn't necessarily all true. If I look back at our relationship, it was me who wanted to be married to him. I wanted him to save me from myself and I thought that he could, but the truth is that only I can do that. Nobody else, just me.

Roger then asked, 'Where has this come from? I knew we were unhappy but this is outrageous.'

I didn't have one rational thought, nothing good to say at all. I'd gone way past the point of breaking the news gently. 'No, it's not. I hate you and I want you out of my house,' I said.

'Where will I go?'

'I don't care. Get out, get out.' I knew I was treating him really badly, but it seemed to be the only way I could find the strength to do it. If I hadn't, I would still be in that bad marriage, too weak and pathetic to do anything about it.

Roger had taken the hint: he packed his things and left. The following morning, he rang me. I apologised to him for the way I spoke to him and said that I'd been trying to tell him for some time and it had all built up inside me. But I soon wished I'd never bothered trying to be nice by explaining myself to him, because he said, 'You can't live without me, you're too weak.' Those words left me very disappointed that Roger hadn't changed at all. He was still the self-centred, lying, manipulative cheat that I'd found out about a few years back.

During that conversation, I turned and looked at our children, and I couldn't help thinking, It's just you and me now, girls. Yet I felt a sense of guilt for what had happened. I'd promised myself years ago that when I married I would make sure that he was Mr Right and, although I didn't want children, if I did have any I would stay in the marriage through thick and thin, as long as he never tried to harm my children. I used to tell myself that would be the only reason I would leave, but that wasn't the case and in only a few years I had contradicted my beliefs.

I don't believe I was wrong to change my views. I was learning how to live like a normal human being and not the animal that I'd been treated like all my life. I knew that I was in the real world with real feelings and I slowly came to realise that those feelings could be hurt very badly. I was no longer switching off but learning to really feel love, hurt and pain. I always tried to distract myself from a problem by creating another one, so, for once, I wanted to get it right.

I'd started to feel very low and I needed some cheering up, so I invited some friends around for a drink and a girlie chat. After quite a few drinks and plenty of talk about men, I started to cry, panicking that I was all alone. 'Linda, I think I'm going to be alone all my life,' I said.

She chuckled and said, 'How do you mean? You've only just thrown him out.'

Then I shouted at her, 'No, you don't get it! I've been alone all my life, thinking I'm in love with people just because they'll have me.'

At this, she stopped smiling. 'What do you mean? You are the most beautiful woman I know.'

I had to explain to her that I wasn't a very happy person inside. 'I've never had much confidence, Linda. I've always put on an act.'

'Well, stop acting and get some, then you might meet the man of your dreams.'

Then it clicked: I *had* met the man of my dreams. 'I think I already have. I just think it's too soon,' I said.

Linda came out with more words of wisdom. 'After everything you went through with Roger — well, just the fact that you told me you haven't loved him for years — I'd say that it probably isn't too soon. Besides, you don't meet the man of your dreams every day.'

I was looking for a reason to call Tyrone and she'd just spurred me along. 'You are so right, I'm going to ring him right now.' I ran to the car, got his number out of the glove compartment and called him, but, when he answered, my nerves got the better of me. I couldn't do it. The words 'far too soon' sprang to mind, and the age difference worried me too. It's not a big gap, only five years, but I had lived a lot for a 23-year-old, and as he was only 18 I thought he might not be able to handle certain things that were going on in my life.

Linda looked very disappointed and told me, 'You rarely meet someone who makes you feel like the age gap is nothing, so make sure you are making the right decision.'

I put my head in my hands, sighed and said, 'I'll think about it overnight. Let's see how I feel when I'm sober tomorrow.'

'OK, Sara, I'm going to go home and let you get some sleep.'

Linda left and I went to bed, but I couldn't sleep. At five

o'clock, I got up and started cleaning the house, and by ten I'd scrubbed every inch, but nothing had taken my mind off of my troubled marriage and the fact that I thought that I was in love with Tyrone. By midday, I couldn't stop myself from calling him, but when he answered I tried to play it cool and said, 'Guess who?'

To my surprise, he knew it was me. 'Hello, Sara, I'm so glad you rang me back. By the way, was that you last night?' He had me sussed, so I admitted to calling him.

'Yes, it was. I'm so sorry but my nerves got the better of me.'

He was very understanding, and said, 'Don't worry about it. I know it's hard for you. Anyhow, how are you?'

'I'm fine.'

We spoke for two hours and I was so happy to carry on talking that I was walking around the kitchen balancing the phone on my shoulder while putting out the kids' dinner and washing up. I enjoyed our conversation so much, I asked him, 'Would you like to come round to mine for supper tonight?'

'Yes, thank you. I'll see you at...?'

'Nine. I'll put the kids to bed first.'

I then rang Linda to fill her in on the latest bit of gossip and she was so happy for me she offered to have the kids overnight. I began rushing round like a mad woman, packing the kids' toys, throwing the bags in the car and telling the kids their bedtime story on our way over to Linda's. She was waiting for me at the door and said,

'Give 'em here, hurry up, go on. I'll see you later. Have a great time, and good luck.'

I had no time to spare. I'd just grabbed a shower when the doorbell rang. Tyrone was standing there with a bottle of wine and some chocolates, and then he put his arms around me. It felt great, but he apologised. 'Sorry, Sara, I couldn't help myself. I've wanted to hug you since the moment I clapped eyes on you.'

He hadn't offended me at all. I really enjoyed having someone to hold me, someone who made me feel special, for the first time in a very long while. We talked for hours and the more I got to know him, the easier my love came for him. I fell in love that day, and from then on we spent as much time together as possible. Because our relationship progressed so quickly, I soon introduced him to my family. That day, Mum took one glance at him, then looked as though she was ready to pass out. She called me to her room and said, 'I thought you said he was black.'

'He is,' I replied. 'His dad's half-Chinese, half-Jamaican. His Mum's white. I know he looks white, but you would have to see his dad to understand why he's so light-skinned.' There I was again, apologising to her for dating someone who wasn't quite up to her standards. Not that she truly had any: she was the type who made it up as she went along.

I soon got fed up with the horrible things that she often said about Tyrone when she rang me at home. It was a rare thing for my mother to call me, but she had no choice as I had stopped visiting her so much because of her rude attitude towards my new partner. I could guarantee that whenever she'd call she would ask how Porky was. I knew she wasn't referring to his weight because he was tall and slim, but was talking about his skin colour. She wouldn't even let it drop when I was pregnant with our first child Nicola. She'd often say, 'You do realise that your baby will come out white, don't you?'

I'd hear those words from her at least once a week, as though I was supposed to be worried more about the baby's skin colour than if it came out healthy, with all its fingers and toes. Not once did she ask how my pregnancy was going, how I was feeling or about my plans for the birth, like a regular mother would. She would try to put a damper on the whole thing by trying to make me believe that having a child with someone with a different complexion to myself and my siblings was a terrible crime and I was very wrong to be doing so.

Tyrone had changed dramatically over the months leading up to the time for me to give birth to our first child. He had started drinking heavily and I noticed he would come home late more and more often, and with bruises all over him. Sometimes he had grass stains all over his clothes from where he had fallen over. The police brought him home a couple of times too. Before then I'd not worried that he liked a drink, although it bothered me a little because I knew that we both came from families of heavy drinkers. Earlier, I'd thought nothing of it, but now it was different, and I told him so.

'Tyrone, I'm worried that you're turning into an alcoholic. Could you please cut down on your drinking?'

His response was, 'Fuck you, you fucking bitch.' Kick! Punch!

He had beaten me for speaking my mind and I called the police, who took him away, leaving me baffled and wondering if I should have waited until he was sober to talk to him. Only minutes after he'd gone, my waters broke. Nicola wasn't due for another month but Tyrone's behaviour had sent me into early labour. I rang the police and asked them to send him to the hospital because I was in early labour. By the time he got there, I was in full labour and I grabbed him around the neck and almost strangled him while trying to push our child out. I'm still not sure if I was doing it because it was helping me get through the pain, or if I was trying to kill him for putting me though all the things he had.

Ten minutes after he'd arrived, Nicola was born, my fourth little girl. He started crying and grovelling, 'I'm so sorry, Sara, I am. Please forgive me.'

Stupidly I said, 'It's OK, Tyrone. Look at her, she's beautiful. I love you.'

I was so relieved to have got through it all in one piece, and to see that our daughter was so healthy, that what had happened in the past between us didn't seem to matter any more. I truly believed that we could both move on with our gorgeous daughter and hoped that things would change.

My mum had asked me if she could be at the birth because she couldn't wait to see what colour the baby was. That was when I realised that I'd had enough of her and her ridiculous opinions. I finally stood up to her. Well, not quite: I got Tyrone to pretend that it all happened so fast that we didn't have time to call her. It wasn't exactly a lie – it did happen very fast – but I also made him wait three hours after the birth before he called her. She came rushing to the hospital, of course. The way she stormed into the room and ran over to the cot made my skin crawl. 'Hello, Sara. Wow, she's darker-skinned than I thought she'd be.'

I took one look at her and said pointedly, 'Yes, she's beautiful too, isn't she?' But my sarcasm didn't seem to register at all and she kept on and on about how well she'd tan as she got older and that her skin colour could possibly get darker, while she was checking the tips of Nicola's fingers to see if there were any signs of her skin getting darker. I was so upset by her thoughtless behaviour that I turned away and said I was tired, in the hope that I'd get rid of her.

When at last she left, I found myself apologising to Tyrone for how racist my mother had been. It was weird to have to do that, especially as she was the only white person there. He must have thought she was a crazy woman. Besides, my mother's racist comments after the birth helped me to forget about what had happened between us earlier that day.

I think my way of dealing with my troubled relationship with Tyrone was to remember the person I met, not what he'd turned into. It was deteriorating at a slow pace, but I refused to give up, always telling myself, 'He's drinking too much – that's why he gets like he does. There's nothing wrong with him when he's sober.'

But I was so wrong; Tyrone had started drinking every day. He'd hurl abuse at me and sometimes cause a fight with me or anyone in the vicinity. One time he beat our neighbour severely for trying to stop Tyrone from attacking me. The police were being called out to the house all the time and my landlords were threatening me with eviction if Tyrone didn't change his ways. My family had found out about it and my brother Carl had given up on me completely. He said he'd had enough of the rumours that were flying around our estate.

On the day we took our daughter home, no sooner had we walked through the door than the phone started ringing. My brothers and sisters called me one by one and they all said words to the effect that, 'Mum said that she's white with a tan. Is it true? I can't wait to see this.'

Funnily enough, their attitude towards the colour of my daughter's skin didn't bother me at all. I had almost expected that kind of reaction, because my mother had always played the puppeteer with me and my siblings. She often allowed them to believe that whatever I was doing at the time was wrong, no matter how pathetic her reasons were. And, although I was the only person who knew the real reason, that she'd raised my brothers and sisters not to respect me or anything that I did, I always went along with her because deep down I was still trying to protect her, in the hope that she'd see that I was willing to let her get away with all of it, because I loved her and wanted her to be a real mother to me.

I'm not even sure if she realised that she was turning them against me to protect herself from the embarrassment and shame that she would have suffered if I'd got too close to my siblings and told them all the stories about my mother and father, and the way she handled his sexual abuse of me. Either she did and she was just an evil woman with no intention of ever trying to rectify her mistakes, or it was in her subconscious and she was in self-protect mode. All I know is that she was starting to cause the biggest rift between them and me; a rift that would never be healed.

18

Mother's Guilt

My relationship with my brothers and sisters slowly deteriorated over the years. I was trying so hard to be close to them, but they always treated me terribly. I found their actions very confusing, because, although they would come to me with every single problem, as though I was their mother, just as soon as they found the opportunity to cause a problem for me, they'd jump on it. There I was constantly trying to help them, hoping that next time they'd see that I was doing so because I wanted us to be close, but they'd always throw my help back in my face.

I started to notice just how much my mother had poisoned them against me on Boxing Day, just six months after I'd given birth to Nicola. I'd just been shopping with the children and Roger. Tyrone and I had split up, because he had started drinking heavily and had got very violent at times. The drastic change in his personality had come as a big shock to me and had left me feeling very disappointed, depressed and alone, because he was my true first love and I had planned on growing old with him. Sad, hurt and lonely, I was at an all-time low.

Roger was trying to cheer me up by joking as we drove to our regular Boxing Day meal at my mother's. He laughed about how I used to be a pain in the arse whenever I had my period and said that he'd never known a woman who suffered from PMT so badly. He said he used to log the dates of my period so that he knew when to steer clear of me. While he was talking, something clicked in my head and I turned to him and said, 'Take me to the chemist's — I think I've missed a period.'

Gobsmacked, he took one look at me and said, 'Oh, my God, are you sure? Do you know how late you are?'

I couldn't remember but I knew that it was best to find out as soon as possible. Because of the way my relationship with Tyrone had deteriorated, I knew that an abortion was definitely on the cards, and that if I was going to go through with a termination I had to do it quickly, so that I didn't have time to think about it and change my mind. We bought the test kit and went straight to my mother's house. Roger was just as eager to find out the result as I was and asked me to do the test there. I was a bit nervous about doing it at my mother's

house because I wasn't sure how I'd react if I got the
result that I didn't want. Besides, I knew that if I was
going to have a termination it was best if neither of them
knew about it.

But I couldn't wait either, so I ran to the bathroom
and started to do the test. Within seconds, the dreaded
result came up. I sat there in disbelief for a few
minutes. I was in so much shock that I forgot that the
test was on the top of the toilet and the lock on the
bathroom door was broken. Just as I went to pick it up,
my sister Louise burst into the room. 'Oh, my God, is
that what I think it is?' she said, her face beaming with
delight, which told me that she couldn't wait to spread
the news. After all, she was known as 'the news of the
world', the nickname my brother and I had given her
because of her many attempts to spread our problems
around the family.

Grabbing her by the arm, I begged her, 'Louise, don't
tell anyone, please don't. I'm going to have to go
through with an abortion, so I'd rather nobody knew
about it.'

She promised me that she would keep it a secret and
we went downstairs. I whispered the news to Roger and
it was only a few seconds later that I heard Louise
shouting at my mother. I went into the kitchen, where
they were, and said, 'Oh, Louise, it's Christmas. Can't we
all get along for one day?' I wished I'd not said anything
to her when she snapped back, 'Oh, fuck off! Is it your

fucking hormones or something?' I asked her to leave it, but she was on a roll and wasn't going to stop for anything or anyone.

'Oh, don't worry, 'cos you'll be flushing your sprog down the toilet this time next week and then you'll feel better again, won't you?'

Everyone was silenced by her evil tongue. The room came to a halt, with everyone glaring at one another. My heart sank, my mind was racing. I couldn't believe a person could be so cruel.

She must have noticed the anger on my face because she started to run towards the stairs, but I wasn't going to attack her. I'd never attacked any of my siblings – the thought had never crossed my mind – but when she started running I automatically ran after her. All of a sudden, everyone was shouting and trying desperately to stop me, but it was too late. I'd already crossed a point of no return. I was already as angry as a raging bull and before I knew it I was punching and kicking, not realising at the time that it was my mother that I'd hit, until I heard her screams.

Then something clicked in my mind and I stopped myself before I hurt her even more than I already had. Roger grabbed me by the arm and took me away from the house, kicking and screaming. We left before matters got any worse and later that day I rang my mother to apologise for hitting her. She said it was fine and she understood, so I thought that would be the end of the matter.

Mother's Guilt

The following day, Carl was at my door, shouting at me that I was out of order for hitting his mother. I tried to explain to him that I'd done it by accident, but he wasn't listening to me. Fortunately, Roger was there at the time and he told Carl to leave before he lost it too. He explained that I was going through hell and that it was best that they all leave me alone for a while. But Carl didn't want to hear this and left as angry as he had arrived.

Later that day, I received many phone calls from my family. They were all jumping on the bandwagon. After that, they started calling me at all hours of the night for no apparent reason and would come out with the most outrageous comments. Sometimes, the calls would be threatening and very abusive. Because of his guilt about how he had treated me during our marriage, which he often admits, I had a lot of support from Roger, but he often had to go away to work for weeks, sometimes months, so there were many times still when I felt very much alone.

It was at those times that I would take Tyrone back into my life, then have to face the consequences, sometimes within a few days, of letting him back into my home. His physical violence towards me got so bad that I knew that a termination was my only option. After all, having one child by him was bad enough, but I felt that having another child at that time would have kept me tied to him for an awful lot longer, because I wasn't sure if I could stay away from him while I was carrying his child. I believed in the family too much for me to do that, especially as that was all that I ever wanted: a happy home with happy children and a loving partner. But I certainly wasn't getting that from Tyrone; he was too wrapped up in his alcoholism to see what he could have had with me and the girls.

After three weeks of thinking things through, I came to the painful conclusion that an abortion was my only option, so I booked an appointment at the local clinic. But things seldom turn out the way we expect, and the shock that came to me a few days before my appointment was to change everything. My grandfather died suddenly and I became very depressed, lonely and hurt. His death left me wrestling with my emotions and beliefs. On the one hand, I was thinking that it was an appropriate time to go through with a termination because of the pain I was feeling, while on the other hand I felt guilty for contemplating killing my own child when I'd lost someone who meant so much to me to natural causes.

Riddled with guilt, I didn't know which way to turn. I couldn't talk to my mother, not only because she was grieving herself, but also because I still believed that she wouldn't have been interested. I was going through a terrible time! Tyrone was being totally unsupportive and selfish: not once did he consider my feelings or what I was going through. He was treating me the same as he ever did; worse, if anything.

Mother's Guilt

He had been a complete pig, drinking even more over the days leading up to the funeral. At times, he had been very nasty to me and this made me feel resentful towards him. He didn't understand at all what I was going through. I don't know what happened over those few days after Granddad passed away, but Tyrone seemed to want to hurt me even more than I already was. Maybe he couldn't handle the way it had upset me and the only way he knew how to deal with it was to lash out.

On the morning of the funeral, I stormed out of the house after he kept shouting at me that I had better not stay too long because he had things to do. I knew that he had nothing to do, so I told him to grow up and that he'd picked the wrong day to try to control me. I left the children at home with him, but, when I was only halfway there, he rang my mobile and screamed at me, 'You'd better bring back my fucking money. I need it now, so you'll have to come back.'

I looked in my bag and noticed that, when we'd been shopping the day before to get my suit for the funeral, he'd put his wallet in my bag because he hadn't got any pockets. I panicked and put the phone down on him. I knew that he would have wound himself up otherwise, but after that he kept on calling me. 'Bring back my money now.'

'I can't, Tyrone, I'm on my way to the funeral,' I told him.

Still he kept insisting that I bring it back home, but then said, 'I don't care if you don't bring it back, I'll come up there and fetch it, and you wouldn't want a scene at your granddad's funeral, would you?'

I knew he wouldn't have dared cause a scene in front of my family, so I told him, 'I can't be bothered with this. Goodbye, Tyrone.' I was fed up with his games and thought to myself that if he dared come to my nana's house my brother would have him straight away. I went to the funeral without listening to his threats. I still looked out for him the whole time. He had ruined what should have been a special day for me and my family to say goodbye to a loved one. I couldn't stop thinking how evil he was to put me in that position on that particular day. His behaviour left me feeling so wound up that I went home straight after the funeral to confront him. He had spoiled a very emotional time for me, to the point where I still feel as though I haven't said goodbye to my grandfather properly because of him.

I tried to talk to him, but we argued for hours. Being his usual selfish self, he was determined to break my heart. I wanted to hurt him so badly that my hormones were racing all over the place. My sole thought when I saw him was, I hate the bastard. I'd already lost the only man that I'd ever trusted fully and that was the day that I knew that I was losing the love of my life too. He'd changed and I didn't even like him any more, let alone love him.

Tyrone knew that I was weak and vulnerable and he used that fact to his full advantage. I told him, 'I hope you lose someone very close to you, then maybe you'll know exactly how I feel.' But he angered me even more when he said, 'I won't act as pathetic as you.' God, if only he'd known that it was not an act. I *was* in pain.

Only a few days after that argument, his grandmother died. There had been no sign that she was ill; she just passed away suddenly. I felt very cruel for the things that I'd said, but I thought that maybe now he would know how it felt and be able to understand my grief. He was beside himself with grief; he even apologised to me for the things he had said and done since my granddad had died. He was finally feeling pain and he cried in front of me for the first time ever. We were close again. We'd both been through a lot and were starting to understand each other.

His grandmother's sudden death had made him think about the amount of alcohol he had been consuming and he told me he wanted to give up. He felt worried, he said, about dying from alcohol poisoning, but his words turned out to be just that – words! As soon as his grandmother's funeral was over he started drinking heavily again. I knew it wouldn't last long, but I hoped it would. I'd had enough, so I told him that he had to find somewhere else to live, and that until he did I would be sharing Nicola's room with her.

Although I had the kids and Tyrone, I was very much alone again. It got to the point where I felt as though I was sleeping with my enemy but too scared to put a stop to it. So when, only four months after Nicola was born, I fell pregnant again with my fifth child that would be born into a bad relationship, I decided to see the doctor about a termination. However, after my grandfather's funeral, I had a change of heart and decided that I wanted to keep the baby. It was a very hard decision, but I couldn't go through with an abortion at a time like that. Besides, I didn't want one. The only reason I was considering it was Tyrone's appalling behaviour.

As the months went by and I was getting closer to giving birth to our baby, I wanted to be close to him again, because I needed someone to talk to, and whenever he was sober, which admittedly wasn't very often, I saw a very different side to him. Sometimes the old Tyrone came back and I often wanted him to stay. We started to make a go of things again, only this time I decided I was going to ignore any mistakes he made and try to get on with our lives. I was so blind to it all that I only started to have reservations about our relationship lasting much longer after Paige was born.

I was feeding her during the night, when I caught him almost urinating over both of us as he stumbled drunkenly over the bed. What scared me the most was the fact that he denied the whole thing and did so almost every night. For quite a while, he would urinate over the wall or sometimes in the bed, but if ever I confronted him he'd tell me I was a liar, while insisting that I was putting water there to try to send him mad. He wouldn't listen to me at all, so again I moved into the other bedroom, but I knew that he resented it and it would be only a matter of time before he did or said something about it.

I was right again. Days later, at five in the morning, I could hear him making his way towards my room. He had a big plastic smile on his face when he said, 'Hello, darling, have a drink with me.'

I replied, 'No, Tyrone, some of us have to get up in the morning. If I don't, are you going to take the kids to school?'

That's when he flipped, shouting, 'Shut up and have a drink. Have a fucking drink.' He threw the drink in my face and wouldn't let me get up to get a towel. He kept on shouting while holding me down by my throat. 'You are never getting rid of me, no way. You are mine.'

There was no point in struggling. I knew what he was about to do. I'd seen that look many times before. I could see it in his eyes, but I was too scared and too weak to fight him off. When he started tearing off my clothes and clumsily lying all over me, I couldn't breathe properly. The only thought racing around my mind was, Why is this happening again?

While he was violently raping me, I could see that he hadn't a single thought in his head about what I'd been through in the past. I lay there and wished him dead, wished he would choke on his own vomit or have a heart attack while having his fit of rage. I hated him. The following morning, while he was in his drunken sleep, I left the house for good. I went to a friend of his father's. His dad had lots of properties that he rented to various people. I hoped that he'd help me, so I told him the entire truth, everything that Tyrone had done, including the rape.

Normally, I would never have told anyone about my home life. I used to be so secretive when it came to Tyrone's behaviour because he had drummed it into my head that I talked too much. I realise now that he didn't want me telling anyone about what went on behind our door, because he had something to be ashamed of, but at the time I took in what he said because I was always trying to prove that I was the opposite of what he thought of me. I suppose he was manipulating me and I didn't even realise it, so telling Bruno everything was a big breakthrough for me. I had proved to myself that I meant business, and there was no going back.

Bruno was so disgusted that this young man whom he'd known since he was a child, and had even babysat at times, had turned into a little monster. He helped me by getting a few of his friends together to watch Tyrone's every move. Once Tyrone left the house to go to the pub, one of them followed him there and the others went with a big van to get all my stuff out of the house. They managed to get almost everything before Bruno's friend called and said that Tyrone was on his way back. It was fantastic, because now I could start afresh without having to worry about having to buy new stuff for my new house. But the most important thing was the fact that I'd finally escaped Tyrone and his controlling ways.

19

Help at Last

With plenty of support from Bruno, I very soon settled with the children into our new home. But after the rape I knew that I could possibly be pregnant, so, as soon as I'd sorted out the kids, I went to the local chemist and bought the morning-after pill. It had been 42 hours since the rape and so I knew that I had to hurry because I only had another day to take it. I went and got the pill on time, but I had to be one of that one per cent that it didn't work for! Three weeks later, I had a positive pregnancy test again. He'd raped me and invaded my privacy and the result was another unwanted baby. I thought back to when I first considered a termination, when I was pregnant with Paige. It was still fresh in my mind as it was only 11 months earlier. I decided there was no point in seeing a doctor about a termination. I knew that I would end up choosing to have the baby and that I was going to have to do it by myself.

I'd been to every doctor's appointment by myself and at my 20-week scan they told me that I was having a boy. I felt so excited I nearly wet myself. My first little boy. I couldn't believe it when they told me that he might have a problem with his heart. I didn't know how much more I could take and I thought to myself, It's always the way. If I get good news, it's always followed by something bad. I needed to talk to someone, but I believed that my family wouldn't understand, because I'd always played it tough around them. I rarely let them see my weak side: I suppose it was my way of protecting them from feelings of guilt after what my dad did to me. I started to wish that I could talk to Tyrone, but I knew that I couldn't. For one thing, he didn't even know about the baby and anyway we hadn't had any contact since the day I left the house, so I kept it to myself and waited until my 34-week scan.

The weeks went by very fast. It was almost Christmas and I had such a lot to do. I hate Christmas shopping, but I had no choice but to try to get some of it out of the way, so I went out to the local shops. I began to wish that I'd chosen another day when I bumped into Tyrone's mother in the supermarket. 'Hello, Sara, how are you? I need to talk to you, can we go somewhere to sit down?'

I thought she was going to ask me to let Tyrone see the kids, or tell me how well he was doing with giving up alcohol or something. I certainly didn't expect to hear what I did that day. I agreed to talk to her. 'Yes, of course we can.'

'Sara, it's bad news,' she said.

There were tears in her eyes, so I snapped at her in a panic, 'What is it?'

'Tyrone died two weeks ago.'

My heart sank. 'What? How?'

Her eyes had such a painful expression when she told me, 'He choked in his sleep.'

I felt guilty for not being there for him. I also remembered wishing for that very thing to happen many times in the past and blamed myself for wishing him dead. I started to apologise. 'I'm sorry, I'm so sorry, I thought that if I left him he would sort himself out.'

'It's not your fault. We all knew he'd been heading that way for a long time, didn't we?' I knew she meant well but I couldn't handle what she had told me, so I tried to make my excuses and leave. 'This is all too much. I can't talk right now. Can I call you later?'

'Yes, of course you can. But wait, Sara, one thing, is that baby you're carrying Tyrone's?' I hesitated to tell her the truth, not because I didn't want her to know but because I'd kept it a secret from his family for so long that I had programmed myself not to say anything. 'Yes, it's a boy,' I said. As we sat there, both of us in tears, we couldn't look at each other. I had to get out of there, so I grabbed my stuff and started running so fast that I couldn't keep up with myself. Suddenly, I fell to the ground. When I stood up, I was surrounded by a pool of water. I sat back down and screamed, 'Why? He didn't deserve to die.' I was angry with the world and thinking how easily it could have been me.

To this day, I still believe that Tyrone was going through some serious issues in his mind, because as a child he too was abused for a short time by his older brother. He often told me that he felt disgusted with himself and he never told a soul in case the person he told thought that he was gay, because he was ashamed that it was a man who had abused him. He also watched his parents get drunk every night and fight like cat and dog. He wasn't to blame for his actions: he had a lot of issues to deal with. He should have got help but he never did, and that was the only way he was to blame.

I know that I left him, but I always secretly hoped that he would find himself, get better, then make contact with us and we'd live happily ever after. But that day I had to face the fact that I would be alone forever and that he would never be there for us again. I went into labour within minutes of my waters breaking. I raced home to call Linda to ask her to come over and look after the children for a while. I put off going to the hospital for as long as I could, because I was scared. I still didn't know if my son's heart would be OK, and I was only just 34 weeks pregnant. In the end, it was Linda who called the ambulance. She went ballistic at me, telling me to pull myself together for my son's sake. I was so lucky to have her there, whereas my family was of no support to me whatsoever. They have never understood what it took for me to get where I am today. They all think that I'm as tough as old boots. If only they knew the truth.

The ambulance arrived just in time and my baby arrived just five minutes after we got to the hospital. Little Kyle was a healthy 5lb 13oz. They told me that his heart was healthy, and so was he in general, considering he was six weeks premature. I was even more surprised when they told me that we could go home the following morning. I felt so lucky to have him, especially after worrying for so long that he'd be born with health problems, but he was a greedy little fighter, just like his mum!

I couldn't sleep that night. I thought of Tyrone every time I looked at my son's face. I blamed myself for his death, often wondering whether, if I'd begged him to get help, he would still be alive. He would have loved that moment, too: a baby boy, such a special day for both of us. I kept myself from going insane by believing that Tyrone could see us, telling myself he was around there somewhere, but I wished I could see him just one last time.

The following morning, after Kyle had seen the paediatrician, they told me I could go home. Linda and the kids came to pick us up. It was Christmas Eve and I'd not got much done for Christmas, but the girls didn't mind; they were just pleased to have a new baby brother. I decided not to tell them about Tyrone until after the

New Year, as I didn't want to ruin their holiday, but it was so hard keeping a secret like that because I kept breaking down. And, whenever they asked me what was wrong with me, I lied, telling them that it was all down to the baby blues.

On Christmas Day, at five o'clock in the morning, I sat on the sofa with my newborn baby in my arms, watching the kids open their presents, trying to smile and look happy, but my feelings of guilt were making me cry. I felt very bad for our daughters and our new baby son, being the only person knowing that they would never spend Christmas with their father again, and they didn't even know it, and the worst aspect of it all was that they were too young to have any memories from the past. All they had to remember him by was a few old photos.

It somehow felt worse knowing that Roger would be picking up my older three girls after dinner. They had their dad to spend Christmas with and fortunately they were very close to him. But it didn't help knowing that, because my three younger children would never again have that chance. Luckily, they never saw a negative thing that went on between Tyrone and me, so they don't know what a monster he became towards the end. I felt better knowing that at least I could tell them nice stories about him and they'd never have to know the truth.

That day felt like the worst Christmas I'd ever had, even compared with those I'd spent as a child with my father. It even topped the time when my brother Carl had got a dartboard from my grandfather for Christmas and my dad pinned us all up against the wall and threw darts at us because we'd accidentally made a tiny hole in the wall. That was a very painful experience, but nowhere near as painful as lying to my children. It hurt me so much to lie to them, especially as I'd promised myself I never would. So when Jasmine started asking questions I almost broke down and told them the truth. 'Mum, why are you crying?' she said.

'Jasmine, I'm very tired, but I'm also very happy. I am very proud of you all and I love you all very much, and having baby Kyle has made it even better.' I felt totally disgusted with myself when she reached out to me for a hug and said, 'Oh, Mum, come here.'

When they all joined in on a group hug I almost told them, but I managed to bite my lip. We got through that Christmas without any more tears. I stayed strong for my kids by putting it all to the back of my mind. But come January, I decided it was time to tell the girls about Tyrone's death.

As I sat them down, I couldn't help thinking that I was doing something wrong. I felt as though I was about to break their hearts and there was nothing that I could do to stop it. I knew it had to be done. I'd promised myself years earlier that I would never lie to my children. I've always asked them to be honest with me, so I believe I owe it to them to do the same. After all, I never had that kind of relationship with my parents, so it's been very important to me in my children's upbringing. As the words left my lips, the three older children broke down in tears. They fully understood what had happened, especially as we had only lost Granddad a couple of years before.

Yet Nicola and Paige were asking me for chocolate and skipping around without a care in the world. They didn't understand. I should have been happy for them, but the reality of it was that I knew that they would have to go through it all again in years to come. I knew that would be when they would suffer the pain of not being able to see their father ever again. What hurt the most was the fact that they never really knew him, and they never would. As the weeks went by, Jasmine, Toni and Beth were slowly getting over Tyrone's death. Roger had been spending more time with them, trying his hardest to help them overcome it all.

I had started to cope better too, feeling stronger and more confident. I had no choice, because I needed to be strong for my children. They needed me, they didn't ask to be born, so I had to raise them, which meant putting all my effort into them and not worrying about the past. All of that went well until another bombshell hit us.

20

Troubled Times

I was becoming very worried about Kyle's health. He had been very sick, throwing up a lot and looking very pale. He looked so ill that I had taken him to the doctor's about nine times in three days, and they kept on telling me that he was fine and that it was just a cold. By early February, I'd just about had enough of the doctors fobbing me off with the same old story. Kyle had been ill for a week and seemed to be getting worse, so I ignored what the doctors had said and called an ambulance for him. His right arm was twitching and it scared me.

The ambulance driver noticed his greyish skin tone and asked me if he was normally that colour. I think I was in denial because I told him I wasn't sure. I knew he wasn't normally grey, but I didn't want to face up to the fact that he was so ill.

At the hospital, the nurses took Kyle straight into the assessment unit. I wasn't sure of what was going to happen but I felt very scared when I saw the doctor approaching me, especially when I noticed tears in her eyes. I knew it could only be bad news. As the words came from her mouth, 'Kyle is very tired. We're going to have to take him up to intensive care,' I went into shock but managed to ask, 'Tired? What do you mean, tired?'

She was trying her hardest to put it to me gently, but I just wanted to know the truth.

'We can only see how he goes through the night, because his right lung has collapsed and he is very weak,' she explained.

Those words brought my whole world crashing down and, although they were throwing hot blankets over me, I couldn't stop shaking. I was in a daze, staring at my son, wondering why God would want to keep punishing me, wondering what I'd done to deserve what was happening and why it had to happen to my son. I wished so hard it could have been me lying there that I started throwing up.

Going down on my knees, I begged the nurse to help him, saying, 'He can't go now, I don't even know him, he hasn't lived. I haven't seen him smile properly yet or walk and talk. Why? Why?'

She took my hand and said, 'You have to calm down: he needs you to be strong. Don't fall to pieces, for Kyle's sake. He's in the best hands, I can promise you that.'

But her words meant nothing because I felt helpless. It was as though my baby had already died. I told myself that he would. I believed so, because I felt that for me luck was non-existent and someone was punishing me by taking away the things that mattered to me the most. Not being able to hold my child was killing me inside. I just wanted to pick him up and take him home to die among all his family.

But I couldn't because he was covered in tubes. They were sticking out of him from just about everywhere on his little body. He was crying but I couldn't hear him because they had stuck a feeding tube down his throat. Not being able to hear him cry hurt the most, because I believed that, if he was going to die and if I was never going to hear him speak, then at least I should have been able to hear him cry one last time.

The doctor asked me to leave while they changed his tube. He believed it would have been too upsetting for me to watch. It surprised me when he asked, 'Aren't you going to kiss Kyle before you go?'

I didn't want to touch him. I'm not sure if it was because I was so numb or if I was scared that I'd hurt him, but I'd programmed myself to leave him alone. I turned around and gave Kyle the most pathetic kiss I've ever given my children – because I didn't want to. It felt like the last kiss I would be giving him and I didn't feel that a goodbye kiss was appropriate. Instead, I wanted to hold him and cuddle him, tell him how much I loved him.

As I left the room, my anxiety was overwhelming. I ran to the chapel to beg for his life. I'm not religious at all and I felt like a bit of a hypocrite, especially as I'd known people who are religious and they had told me that I would turn to God one day if I really needed him. At the time, I thought they were just trying to change my mind, but that day I knew exactly what they meant. Sitting there, all that I could think of was Tyrone. In my mind, I was saying, 'Tyrone, please don't let them take him away. He's too young. I need him, please! He's my baby. What has he done wrong? If there is a God, why doesn't he take the bad people, not my innocent baby boy? Tyrone, don't let them do it, please, I'm begging you.'

Although I felt at ease sitting in the chapel, I couldn't stay there any longer. I needed to get back to Kyle, so I raced back to the unit and didn't move out of my seat all night. The following morning, he was still alive. I kept asking the doctor if he knew what his chances of survival were, but he kept on trying to put things to me gently, by answering in doctor's language. 'Well, he has done well so far, but we have to give him a blood transfusion as his salt and potassium levels are very low and we need to get that sorted before we look at any other problems. He is on an intravenous drip for his antibiotics, so let's hope that they are working.'

I didn't understand half of what he told me, and in my eyes he just hadn't answered my question, but I had to trust the staff; they had to know what they were doing. I was so nervous that I wouldn't leave the ward to call home. I'd left Linda with all the children and I'd not left a penny for her to get anything she needed from the shops.

I became so desperate to use the phone that I begged the nurses to let me use the one on the desk in the ward. They assured me that Kyle would be fine and that I was to use the payphone that was just outside the ward. But, even though I knew I'd only be a minute or two, I needed confirmation that they'd let me know if there was any change. 'Will you come and get me if he gets any worse?'

The nurse frowned at me. 'Yes, of course we will. You won't be gone that long. Don't worry. You need to be strong.'

What if he dies while I'm gone? I kept thinking as I ran to the phone. I'll never forgive myself! That call was the fastest I've ever made. Everyone was fine and that was all I needed to know. I ran back and found them all surrounding Kyle. I went into shock again and screamed across the ward, 'I thought you said you would come for me.'

A nurse ran towards me, saying, 'Shush, he's fine. We're doing his blood transfusion. Don't worry. You signed for it, remember?'

I often went into fits of panic like that over the following three days, until Kyle started to show signs of recovery. He left the intensive care unit on his fourth day there. Then he was transferred to another regular ward for the following six days, and even when it was obvious that he was getting better I kept on telling myself that he would die. I had a terrible shock only days before, and I think that I was convinced that matters could only get worse. Once he was on the ward, I started noticing other mothers' and fathers' pained faces. I knew that they were so sad because they were not taking their child home ever again, and that was when I felt so guilty that I was still worrying over Kyle's health. I felt selfish and ungrateful when I saw that they were in so much pain that I started trying to hide my face whenever I was around them, and even though I'm not religious I used to pray for all of us in the chapel.

It was so strange when I would go and pray because, on the one hand, I was asking God for help, and on the other I kept asking, If there is a God, why does this have to happen? How can he take away young children, some not even a week old? My heart truly went out to those mothers and fathers who were suffering the loss of a child. I can safely say that the intensive care unit is the worst, most traumatic and heart-rending part of a hospital. I never want to have to go back there and hope I will never have to. I take my hat off to all doctors and nurses, who have to look death in the face every day of the week.

On Valentine's Day, after ten days in the hospital, I could finally take Kyle home. I asked Linda to keep the children for one more night at her house, so that I could be alone with him, because I believed we had some serious bonding to do. Although I felt tired, I couldn't put him down all night. I sat and held him in my arms to make up for lost time. I couldn't stop telling him how much I loved him and how proud I was of his strength and the way he survived his ordeal. I felt like the luckiest woman alive to have him there with me. I cherished every second we had.

21

Closure

By the end of that year, Kyle was growing into a healthy toddler. After a lifetime of hurt and pain that had left me totally exhausted, I'd gone through feelings of self-blame, which had often led to self-harm. I'd started drinking heavily and frequently crying myself to sleep, feeling alone raising six children and trying my hardest to cope with simple daily chores. I had become someone I didn't even know any more. I needed some answers and so I went looking for them, first by going to see my father's sister. I hadn't seen Cassandra since I was a very little girl, but I needed to ask her about my childhood and ask her to confirm if all the rumours of incest among the family were true, because, if they weren't, maybe all the things that had gone on were my fault.

I had such stupid thoughts that I even questioned whether I could have encouraged my father to do what he did to me. I just needed to make sense of it all, because I was starting to feel dirty again. I don't know why the whole thing kept on coming back to me, but it did. I suppose that every time my life was in ruins I always thought of the worst thing that had happened to me and blamed my childhood for everything. I wasn't surprised when Cassandra told me that Luther had sexually abused her too, and Ray, my father, had tried to rape her when she was 12. It was confirmed: they all treated their kids like that. I wasn't alone, it wasn't just me. It sounds crazy, but I'd started to think that I was the only person on earth who had been treated that way by her own father. But, once I knew that I wasn't alone, I felt better.

I should have known by then that I wasn't to blame, but I often blamed myself for everything, because I had nobody telling me otherwise. If I ever tried to discuss my past with anyone, they would tell me to stop discussing it, as though I was disgusting. They used to say that they didn't want to hear it because it made them angry. But, whenever they wouldn't listen to me, I felt dirty again. Cassandra's words helped me get through life a little more easily. I knew that I didn't need to blame myself any more. I even opened up and told Cassandra about my uncle Joel. It felt good to get the words out, to say that he also used to rape me when I was a little girl. I had put it to the back of my mind until that day. I'd completely forgotten about it, but all the talks we had about incest in the family brought it back to me.

I suppose it had always been there subconsciously, so getting it out of my system lifted a big burden. When I talked to Cassandra, telling her that I could still remember the smell of his room because he used to wet the bed at the age of 16, she nodded her head and agreed, then told me that she'd been molested by him too. Joel probably wet the bed at that age because he was still receiving a daily beating from his parents, so I somehow didn't blame him for what he had done to me. He was still young then and had taken incest to be a normal part of growing up. I used to put it down to the things he'd seen and the fact that he was so young. Silly, I know, but I had to look at it like that because remembering that I'd been abused by yet another person would have killed me if I'd looked at it in any other way.

My aunt said she looked at it that way too because she also had been abused by her father and had always thought that to be the worst of the abuse she'd suffered. She said that she couldn't blame her brother, because he had only done what he'd seen. Besides, he wasn't her father, and she said that her father hurting her in such a way had got to be the worst form of abuse there is.

I never told anyone else about my conversation with Cassandra, because I thought that they'd think that I was mentally ill and had made it all up, but I was glad that I had been to see her because our talks had enlightened me.

With Ray's family background confirmed to me, I felt I could move on. But I had one more thing to do before that: to confront my father. I believed that by doing this I would be able to help some scars to heal, but part of me didn't want to give him the satisfaction of clapping eyes on me, so I tried very hard to keep away from him.

Because of those feelings, I became very desperate for some company. I needed someone who could understand me and, hopefully, I could look after them too, to give myself some sort of distraction from my past. So that I wouldn't be tempted to go and look for my father and do something that I might regret, I also needed that person to be someone who didn't know everything and was willing to be there for me because he or she loved me. So I asked my youngest sister, Teresa, and her boyfriend to move in with me for a while, to help me get through it all. Teresa was seven months pregnant with her first baby. Her being pregnant gave me something to concentrate on and I enjoyed helping her prepare for the birth, because I believed that babies were something that I specialised in.

I'd only just moved into yet another house, in the hope that I could have a new life without being haunted by terrible memories from the past. I couldn't stay at Bruno's house much longer because I kept on remembering Kyle's illness and the moment when I found out that Tyrone had died.

Teresa's partner was a big lad and I really needed the manpower, so I was very happy when they agreed to move in with me for a while. I also felt comfortable with the fact that Teresa didn't know everything about my past, because she is ten years younger than me and so couldn't remember all that I could. But I soon ruined that safe feeling for myself by getting drunk and crying to her as I told her everything about my mother and father. Although she wasn't surprised at the way my mother handled the whole thing, she wasn't pleased to hear half of the stuff I told her, and on several occasions she asked me to stop. But I was so determined to get everything out of my system that I would go on and on, often crying myself to sleep and having my little sister tuck me into bed.

We became very close and having them stay helped me to get through one of the toughest times of my life, and, although I was creating extra work for myself by having them stay, I really needed the distraction. But then the time was getting close for Teresa to have her baby. When she told me that she would be moving into her new house when the baby came along, I was devastated because, although I love my children dearly, I loved having the adult company around me. Yet, although I felt devastated, I knew that they had to get on with their own lives and be a family. Seeing them together reminded me of what I should have had, and I must admit that, although I felt very happy for them, I was also very jealous, very confused and I couldn't make sense of all the mess I was in.

At that point, I decided to get some help. Teresa suggested that I go to see our sister Kate, who lived across the road from her. I hadn't seen her for years, probably since she was two or three, and not since I used to babysit for Marie when I was 12. It's strange how Teresa and Kate met. All my brothers and sisters look alike, so when Teresa saw her in the street she went over to her and asked her if her father's name was Ray. They quickly discovered that they were sisters and they have been in contact ever since. I considered Teresa's idea for a while, and the more I thought about it, the more appealing it became to me, because I knew that Kate was still in contact with my father. I knew that I would somehow get my chance to confront him and so get some sort of closure on the whole matter.

So I got Teresa to arrange a meeting. I warned her to tell Kate not to tell my dad about the meeting, because I wanted to get to know her a little before I went in with all guns blazing. I was very excited about our meeting and went to see my mum to tell her my plans. She went totally ballistic at me, screaming in my face, 'Why do you want anything to do with those scumbags?' I told her that it wasn't their fault that we had a father like him, but it was too late: she had opened her mouth and I couldn't believe the things that flew out of it. 'You must love it! You must have enjoyed what your dad did to you, you fucking slag. You took my husband away from me and now you want to get to know him again. What about me? I've been left to be a single mother because of you. What about me?'

I could have swung for her, but I tried to explain that I

wanted nothing to do with my father. I told her that I wanted to confront him, if anything. But she kept on coming at me with her outrageous accusations. In the end I walked out, after telling her that she was the most foul-mouthed bitch I'd ever come across and that she'd never see me or my children ever again.

Her words truly hurt me. I'm still angry to this day. I still resent the fact that I've always stood by her, even though I knew deep down that she knew about my father. At times, I was putting her feelings before my own, protecting her as if she was the child and I was the adult. Even when I really needed her, I gave her my all, and, although she'd often given me reason, I never once said anything about the way she handled my father's abuse. Walking out of that house for the last time, I felt so alone, but I knew then that it was for the best. I found the courage to fight back and stop being so soft on the people who had hurt me. I know that my life probably would have been totally different if I hadn't been protecting others instead of myself all those years ago.

Maybe if I had told the truth, the authorities would have done more for me, because she certainly didn't. I would have had appropriate help and more than likely lived a normal life, with no older men, no more abuse. Yes, I would have been taken into care, but a mother like her doesn't deserve children: she is too weak to be the mother she should be. The thought that I've protected her all my life still makes me sick to my stomach. If she'd only been a little more supportive, maybe, just maybe, I wouldn't have spent my life looking for love through other people – mainly men. I would have had love from her and in turn learned to love myself, and I wouldn't have been hurt by so many men.

My mother has never hugged me or told me that she loves me. I think that's the reason why I used to crave love and affection so strongly that I slept with all those men. I needed support after what I'd been through, but she never once gave it to me. She and my father have caused so much damage between them I can never forgive her, especially now that I know she blames me for losing him. When I think about it now, I believe she is just as much to blame as my father was, and, if I hadn't forced her into going to the authorities, she would be with him now.

I went to Kate's flat that night with Kyle, leaving my other children at home with Linda, I didn't want to confuse them, as they were old enough to understand, but I didn't feel ready to talk to them about my father and the number of brothers and sisters I had. As I walked towards Kate's door, I took very deep breaths, feeling very nervous and sick and not quite knowing what to expect. To my surprise, she welcomed me with open arms. We talked about our lives for hours, how many kids we'd had and what a bad hand life had dealt us both. It was great because, although we hadn't spent our childhood together, we had a sisterly bond, and I could feel that straight away. After everything that had gone on, I was very relieved to be getting along with Kate.

Closure

We were sitting there sipping champagne to celebrate our reunion, but it was ruined in an instant when there was a knock at the door and I saw my dad's shadow through the glass. I knew it was him and thought to myself, This is a set-up. 'Why did you tell him, Kate?' I asked.

She looked as shocked as I felt. 'I never told him a thing; it must have been my mum. I thought that I could trust her. Obviously I can't.'

Although I was very nervous, I told her to let him in. Kate looked at me with a confused look on her face and asked, 'Why are you so scared of him?'

I snapped back, 'If you don't know, then I will tell you one day soon.'

As she let him in, I could feel the rage boiling up inside me. I wanted to kill him, and the closer he got towards me, the more I wanted to launch into an attack. Then he spoke. 'Hello, Sara, is that my grandson you're holding?'

The selfish bastard. I couldn't believe he was walking around, acting as though everything was normal, and nothing had happened, so I said, 'Fuck off, Ray. Don't talk to me. I really don't want to have any form of conversation with a freak like you.'

He started laughing. I knew why: he was trying to cover up the shame of what I'd just said to him. I could have smacked him in the mouth when he said, 'You're just like your auntie Cassandra — very rude.'

The cheek! I was so angry you could have cut the atmosphere with a knife. After all the things he'd done to me, he was trying to have a laugh and a joke with me, as though the fact that he'd taken so much of my life was nothing more than taking a child's dummy away when you think they are getting too old to have it. He hadn't taken my dummy: he'd taken not only my virginity but also my sanity, my life, everything that anyone has a right to have.

He then started walking towards Kyle and me. 'Hello, maybe you'll say hello to your Granddad.'

I lost all control. 'You have never earned the right to be called that. If I don't consider you to be my father, then what makes you think that I want my son to call you Granddad? Now get away from him. I hate you. How dare you talk to us! You've got a nerve, you pervert.' I ran out of the door in floods of tears.

Kate followed me and said, 'I think I know why you just acted that way.'

'Why's that then?' I said sarcastically.

'Did he sexually abuse you?' she asked.

And she wasn't surprised when I replied, 'Yes, he did, and the rest. Anyway, how did you know?'

My heart sank when she started to tell me what had happened to her in the past. I began to wish that I'd never asked how she knew, when she said, 'He tried to rape me once, at the park, but I managed to escape. I told my mother but she did nothing, as you can see she's still with him, and so I have to put up with him.'

That's when the confusion set in, for as a mother I wanted to know why these women were letting him get away with his behaviour. Having children of my own, I knew that if a man did that to my girls I'd probably have tried to hurt him in some way. I'd most definitely have left him and the police would have been called straight away. So I asked her, 'Why can't you get away from both of them?'

She replied, 'I have no one else. I need my mum. I'm a single mum and she helps me. Anyway, she's done nothing wrong. She's a good mother and grandmother.'

I was infuriated and asked her, 'How do you work that out? She is standing by a paedophile.'

But she was determined to stick up for her and said, 'She's my mother.'

I begged her to see that she should stay away from him. 'I will help you. Please – get away from them, they're sick! You need to get away, please. I will do anything to help.'

But she didn't understand the severity of his actions and she kept on insisting, 'I can't, my mother would never forgive me.'

I couldn't believe what I was hearing and wanted to get away, so I said, 'Kate, get away from the car. I need to get away from you. You're all crazy.'

I drove off as fast as I could. I wanted to kill Ray for what he'd done. I felt somehow to blame for it all, asking myself why I didn't tell the entire truth in the first place, and telling myself that he would have had a bigger sentence and then maybe he wouldn't have done anything to Kate. The fact that he was still trying to have sex with children made me feel sick. I was alone again with no one to console me or help me make sense of it all. I had to be strong. I needed to calm down and rethink the situation.

After two or three hours of deep thought, I called the local police station that originally dealt with the case. I asked them if there was anything I could do to put a stop to my father's abusive ways. I spoke to someone in child protection and they explained to me that it wasn't my duty to sort him out and that it was down to the people who were still around him. They also explained that I had no evidence of his abuse of my sister and, without a statement from her, there was nothing they could do. I knew Kate would never go to the police about our father, especially considering where she was raised. After all, nobody from around that area goes to the police, no matter what they've had done to them. I decided that my only option was to call Marie and ask her to arrange a meeting between Ray and me. I decided it was about time I stopped worrying about other people and confronted him in front of every person I could, so that he had no way of denying what he'd done.

When I called Marie, to my surprise she agreed to do it, saying that she needed to see it for herself. She told me that hearing about my reaction to seeing him had made her decide that she needed to know the truth, and that she also needed some kind of closure to it all. I asked to talk to Kate and then asked her if she was willing to go to the police with me if I gave her my one hundred per cent support. She refused, as I'd originally thought she would. I was disappointed but thought that I had to confront him myself, and try to move on from it all.

The following day, I made my way over to Marie's house. I walked straight in and started shouting at Ray to tell the truth – for once in his life. He took one look at me and said, 'How dare you talk to your father like that.'

The cheek of the man, I thought to myself, and started to shout as loud as I could, so that the neighbours could hear about the type of man they'd been living near. 'You are not my father. You lost that right many years ago.'

He pulled the face that he used to when he was trying to scare me. 'You are out of order, Sara. Don't talk to your father like that.'

His look didn't scare me at all; it just angered me that he thought he could still manipulate me. 'You – my father? Out of order? No, I'm not, you're a sick man and you need help. Now tell them what you did to me and maybe I can find it in my heart to forgive you enough to say hello to you next time I see you. Maybe I will find a tiny bit of respect for you if you can be a man and tell the truth.'

'I have done nothing to you. You and your mother have ruined my life.'

'You have ruined my life, just by creating me with that bitch of a mother of mine. Now, if Mum and I made this all up, then why – tell me, because I can't work this out – do I hate her too? Wouldn't I be here begging you for forgiveness? Telling you how she'd made me do it and how much I hate her for ruining our relationship. Yes, I hate her, but not because we lied, but because she knew that you were abusing me and did nothing until I forced the issue. Now be a man for once in your sorry life and admit it. Give me some sort of closure. How can you do all the things you've done to your own child and then tell everyone that she's a liar, your own daughter, you sick bastard?'

By now, I could see that devilish look on his face again. His horns came out as he said, 'Don't talk to me like that or I'll...'

I wanted him to bring it on, so I tried to goad him. 'You'll what? I'm not scared of you. I'm nothing like the women you've manipulated all your sorry life. I could never be as weak as them. You see, the one thing you have done for me is make me stronger than them. I would never want to sit back and allow my children to be abused, so I suppose I'm a stronger person than all of you. And remember this, Ray, I was there, I know the truth. You can't convince me you're innocent. You may have got away with it all these years, but the truth is standing here, right in your face. Now I dare you to deny it again. I will tell you this much, I'm not moving until you tell the truth. Be a father for once in your life and give me what I want, instead of taking from me, like you did when you took my virginity at the age of five. I need you to tell the truth. I'm not moving, Ray, not until you own up to everything you've done, and, like I said, I'm not like the others: I'm too strong, mentally and physically, for you to move me.'

I couldn't believe it when he started running away from me. I started to scream at him. 'You weak, pathetic man, you can't even do one thing for your child. After what you did to me, you should be grovelling, begging me for forgiveness. Look at me, don't run away. I need you to tell me that you are sorry and to tell the truth to everyone else.'

I kept shouting at him to stop but he wouldn't, so I grabbed my car keys. I knew what I was about to do, but I couldn't stop myself. I jumped in the car and went after him. Swerving all over the road, I knew that trying to mow him down with my car was wrong, but I had no way of stopping myself. I wanted to hurt him, as much as he'd hurt me all my life. Luckily for me – or him, should I say – I had this little voice in my head that was telling me to stop. The thought of going to prison and leaving my children behind was the only thing that stopped me. Besides, he'd ruined my life enough. I think that I proved my point, which was that he was nothing to be scared of.

I went straight back to Marie's house to tell her what I thought of her. Walking in all fired up, I felt so angry that she would stand by a man who tried to abuse her daughter, especially after he'd been to prison for sexually abusing me and she'd been through the same thing herself with her own father when she was young. She of all people should have known better. I started to scream so loud at her that my throat hurt. 'Marie, do you understand what could have been the consequences of what just nearly happened? I wanted to kill him and, if I had, he could have ruined my life even more than he already has. If people like you hadn't stood by him to the point where you didn't even believe your own daughter, he would have been locked away for good, because he is a sick man. Don't you see that?'

She put her head down, unable to look me in the eyes, and in a very shaky voice started to mumble, 'I wish we'd talked all those years ago. I wish I hadn't gone to stay at your mother's house when I was a child. I wish I'd never met your father. I'm sorry, Sara, I should have been there for you, but he got inside my brain like a cancer and he ate away at it. I'm so glad you confronted him in front of me. I can now see that he is an abusive, lying monster, and I know this because I saw the guilt written all over his face.'

I couldn't help but feel sorry for her. I knew that she was abused as a child by her father too, then she came to us for safety and had been abused by my father ever since. I suppose she was very vulnerable and couldn't believe that he was that way because it was too much of a shock to the system for her. I couldn't help but give her a hug. I thought that I was a weak person but after meeting her again I can see now that I'm very strong, considering my history. I would never let my past affect my parenting. It's a terrible mistake that she made and she's the one who is going to have to live with herself. I walked away from the whole thing, knowing that I didn't need to blame myself for his actions. He is sick, he has a terrible illness, and I don't need to worry any more. It's up to whoever he meets to protect their children. I just have to treat it like dirt off my shoulder, and walk away for good.

Because of that day, I'm now starting to feel some kind of a definitive closure. For the first time in my life, I feel as though someone believes me, and it's not because they are scared of what might happen to them. Some people don't get to confront their abuser, but this is something that I needed to do. But what helped me the most was the fact that I had someone else there to witness his lies, plus the fact that I never told the truth in the first place gave me an even stronger need to confront him. I believed that, if he hadn't terrorised me so much as a child, I may have been stronger as a woman and maybe my life would have been totally different. Maybe I wouldn't have been a single mother at 28 with six children to look after.

I had a lot of hatred and blame for Ray, and I needed to let it out. I cried all the way home, but for the first time in my life it was due to relief and not self-blame and anger. Back at home, giving my kids the biggest hug, I told them they should never hide anything from me and promised them they could confide anything in me, no matter how good or bad. I also promised them that from that day forward their lives would be safe in my hands and that all they needed to do was believe in me. I am there to earn their respect. I brought them into this world and so I truly believe that I have to earn it. As long as fate takes me there, I will be here for them always, and, whatever they need to talk to me about, I will be here. I felt alive for the first time in my life, so excited that I talked the kids to sleep, but it felt OK because, for the first time ever, when I tucked them all in safe and warm, those duvets didn't remind me of my terrible childhood and all the trauma it had brought me.

After that day, my life turned around completely. I no longer looked for love. I learned how to love myself and to be happy within myself. I realised that there is no set time for recovery, no way of knowing how long the pain will be there. The fact that I was nearly thirty didn't mean that I should have dealt with it years ago. I was wise enough to know that abuse is something that you never get over. All people who have been through any form of abuse have to learn to live with it. Especially if the abuser is someone you are supposed to trust and be able to rely on, and even hope that one day will give you away at your wedding. Your own father! A man who should be a fantastic role model and want the best for his children. A man who is supposed to never want his daughter to lose her virginity – well, most hope they'll wait until they're thirty. But that man who is supposed to feel that way took mine when I was five years old. I still find it hard to believe myself.

Yet I finally learned to live and it was like a breath of

fresh air for me. It was almost as though I'd never had room to grow and had only just been born, but born with a great deal of knowledge of life. I learned an awful lot from other people's and my own mistakes, and I feel free to use my knowledge for the rest of my life. I will most definitely use that to the full. I could finally start living without my ghosts following me every step of the way; ghosts that were merely reminding me of all the pain that I had been through; that had, until the moment I confronted my father, kept me feeling like that scared little girl hiding under her duvet. They were gone for good. I had found a way of living, something that at one point in time I thought was totally out of my reach. But, with nothing in my way to stop me, I was finally living for the first time. At last I'd found my soul, which was lost for so long, and it felt great!

22

Finally Happy

Things are really looking up. My life is so different now. Many changes have occurred, yet for once not one of those changes has involved my heart being broken. I've had a few minor ups and downs, but none of them has harmed my household. One might have done, but it turned out all right in the end.

We had a house fire a few months ago and it was terrible at the time because I was sitting on the sofa in my pyjamas when it happened. Only an hour before the fire, I was fitting the last little piece of laminated flooring in my front room. Afterwards, I felt really grubby, so I took a bath and then I was about to relax after two days of hard work, when I heard a loud bang. I ran to the kitchen, opened the door and the tumble dryer was ablaze. I grabbed the kids, put them in the car outside and called the fire brigade. At the time, I couldn't believe it. I'd just finished my house and the floor was the last little touch that I had to add to it, but, just as I relaxed, very pleased with my efforts, it all went up in smoke.

After they'd put out the fire, the firefighters allowed me to go in and collect a few necessities. I walked through the door hesitantly, thinking to myself, God, you're so unlucky, it had to be you. But then I started laughing. That was when I realised that I was lucky! My kids could have been badly injured. If I'd put that machine on at night, things could have been much worse. It was only due to the fact that I wanted everything to be perfect after I'd finished the floor that I didn't wait to get the washing done until later on that night. So I was very lucky. It could have turned out much worse than it did.

But I still couldn't help thinking that I'd lost everything when one of the firefighters said, 'You have such a lovely home. Don't give up. If I were you, I'd sue the company that made your machine. I'll give you a good report and they'll have to cough up.'

Why not? I thought. I'll give it a go. After all, the machine was only a year old, so it must have been faulty. Besides, I had no choice. I had no household insurance because I was always broke and there was no way I'd be able to replace everything that had been damaged. I couldn't even afford a new toaster at the time, so buying new beds and sofas seemed totally out of the question.

Finally Happy

After dropping the kids off at my brother's house, I went back home and started calling solicitors, the manufacturers of the dryer and so on. After I'd told them what had happened, the manufacturers quickly offered to send an engineer out, and then the loss adjusters. It all happened so fast. After only a week, and obviously a quick glimpse at the inside of the machine, they accepted liability. I couldn't believe it. I knew that, once they'd accepted liability, it would only be a matter of proving to them how much that I'd lost and the cheque would be at my door. I found as many receipts as I could, and then I took pictures of the rest of the bits of badly burned furniture, which I'd placed in a gigantic skip outside my house by then. I could never wait to do anything and had cleared the entire house within days of the fire. Patience has never been my strong point.

Three months later, they sent me a cheque for £15,000. I couldn't believe my luck. I'd never seen that much money in one go before, but when I thought about it I knew I had to be careful with the money, because I'd lost much more than that, but I couldn't argue the point with the loss adjusters and the company involved because I needed beds and furniture for my family. If I'd waited much longer, we'd have had to go into a hostel because of the health risks. So, although a bit peeved that I'd spent 12 years struggling to buy nice furniture so that my kids could live better than I did, I took the money. I went out and bought every bargain replacement that I could find. I even managed to get that leather corner unit I'd wanted for so long and thought would never happen. I also managed to get my American fridge freezer, which I'd always thought would only ever be a dream. But fortunately things had gone down in price since I brought my old fridge and it was the same price as the old one. I was so happy!

I managed to get such great bargains that I even had enough money left over to buy a computer for Jasmine. She'd been begging me to get her one for years and I often felt terrible when Christmas came around and she had that look of disappointment on her face. But now she didn't have to be sad ever again, because for once I could afford to buy what she really wanted. I made it an early Christmas present and she was so happy she kept it in her room and stared at it with pride all the time. She loved it and she wrote many stories on it, some so good that she took them into school to show her teacher and often got a gold star for her efforts.

Jasmine was very proud of her writing and, even though I had no knowledge of computers whatsoever, she managed to get me interested in writing too. She taught me how to use the computer, and then one day, while she was at school, I decided to try to write my own life story. I had been told by many of my friends over the years that I should try to write a book. I often thought that they had a point but I shrugged it off and thought to myself, considering I'd never even read a book, that I couldn't possibly dream of offending many writers by trying to do something that they had had years of schooling for and plenty of practice at. But then I've never been one to let formalities stand in the way! So I thought to myself, Even if this is only for me, it could be very beneficial to my healing. As I began to write, suddenly I felt relieved at how easy it was. It was almost like an act of cleansing that made me realise that my story needed to be told. Soon six pages became 12, 12 became 18 and, before I knew it, writing my life story was changing my life forever. I realised that I had a purpose in life.

Many friends read my work and told me I should use it to help others. Linda insisted that I send it off to some kind of organisation, to try to help them. I had no choice but to listen to her, because when Linda has an idea it's best to go with it. If I hadn't, I'd have had to stand the headache for many months to come. So that was when I decided to send my work to my local rape crisis centre. They thanked me for being so open and asked me if it was OK to use it for training their volunteers.

The woman there then told me that I should try to turn it into a book, because my story was so heart wrenching and brutally honest. Again, I went into a panic, telling myself it would be too difficult. But I persevered and before long I was writing all the time. The children were very helpful. Jasmine and Toni desperately wanted me to get published so that they could go to school and tell all their friends. They often told me to go to work and offered to clean the house. Work to them meant the computer in their bedroom. They would tell Roger off for going on about how hard he worked. Jasmine would say, 'Mum has a job too. She works just as hard as you! So you'll have to pick us up from school today.' Never one to mince her words, she definitely takes after me.

I spent many hours writing and rewriting my work in their room. They understood what it took for me to write down my life story and often asked me if I was OK. It's strange when I think about that now, because the girls didn't know the half of it, but what they'd seen was enough to make them understand that it would be hard to write down all those events that had consumed my life for so long.

I'm not ready just yet for the girls to know everything about my life, and I don't think they are either. But one day I want them to know the truth about my past. I think it's better than their not knowing why they don't have anything to do with certain members of their family. After all, most people tell their children about their family history. I honestly believe they should know the truth. Even though it's a terrible story to tell them, kids shouldn't be shielded from the world, and I'm not the type of mother to make them feel that it's a wonderful and safe place, because we all know it isn't. So, when they are ready, I will tell them everything they want to know, but, for now, although I hate not talking to them about it, because it makes me feel like a politician, I'll keep on trying to avoid answering their questions.

Finally Happy

I had some funny times while I was writing. Kyle would run around teasing Nicola, Beth and Paige, and they'd often be asking me for choccy bickies, fizzy drinks and many other things that I'd normally refuse point-blank to let them have, but they asked me knowing that I was distracted and would agree to anything. I'd often wave my hand at them, saying, 'Yeah, yeah, have what you like.'

They'd go running off, happily yelling, 'Mummy said we can have what we like! Yeah.'

They knew exactly when to ask too, but all in all my children put up with my writing and were very helpful.

I often took breaks from it because I didn't want them to feel neglected. That was my only worry while writing. I suppose I'd gone from being a full-time mum to being a full-time but unpaid career woman. Which meant that childminding was out of the question, and having to juggle the two by myself meant that I had to do a lot of thinking and worrying. But it was all worth it and the kids and I had loads of fun while I was writing.

We regularly had days out, which helped me because I was getting a much-needed break from my writing and it also gave us many fun times and good bonding sessions. Our trips to the countryside were the funniest times I can recall. After all those hours sitting in front of the PC, I had a little bit of a rough time running after the children up those hills. I'd often give up and offer to take them to the fair, which cost a packet, but I didn't mind at all. Just the look on their faces was enough to make me forget about the financial side of things for one day.

I saved up for weeks to take them to Weston-super-Mare. We only went for the day but a day was more than enough. I can't believe how tiring taking six little ones out on your own can be. I thought that I was used to it and could handle anything, but, boy, was I wrong. They were running off in different directions, screaming all day, whinging for this, that and the other. I had a terrible time, but they loved it. I felt so special when we all sat down for our picnic, and they all thanked me for taking them on holiday. Part of me felt bad because I wanted to do so much more with them, but two weeks in Spain was totally out of the question; there was no way that our finances would allow for that kind of expense. I'm so happy that my kids can appreciate the little things in life and I know that when I can afford to do more they'll be elated. They could never be spoiled and unappreciative, which is a good thing because I know they'll never expect to have things when they ask and, although they may feel a little disappointed at times, I don't get tantrums and paddies thrown at me.

I love the fact that my girls feel so close to me, and having Kyle is wonderful. I must admit, though, that, with him being the only boy, we girls spoil him rotten! We have a real laugh with him. From the moment he could walk, he loved the girls' pink tutus and feather boas. They would dress him up and he used to love it, but just recently he's noticed the difference and denies ever wearing the stuff. He now asks for boys' toys and won't go near any girls' toys or their fancy-dress outfits.

There's so much love in our house that it's about to burst, and that makes me feel very special. To have achieved something so good, under such terrible circumstances, we are all very happy, and to have happiness, after all that has happened to all of us, is a wonderful feeling.

My writing has sent me in many directions. I have met many survivors along the way, many real people with real stories to tell, many people who haven't yet found their voice and therefore aren't quite ready to talk about their experiences. Some of those people have become very good friends of mine. We have trust, friendship and a very good understanding of what one another has been through in life. Which is why I'm so happy with what I've achieved during the past few years. Before I started writing, I thought that I was doomed to a life of let-downs and failure. Now I can see that there always is a light at the end of the tunnel; it's just up to the individual to find it. A little guidance helps, which is what I will try my best to do for my kids, it's just a pity that my parents didn't try to do the same. But at least I can say that I've broken the cycle. And, in my book, that is a brilliant success in itself.

The End

This story is about my life and how I suffered many pitfalls on my journey towards the steps of the recovery process, after suffering child sexual abuse for many years. Therefore, the events which took place are solely my own and no one else's. I can say after meeting many survivors along the way that everyone's tale is very different. Some have the support of their carers, family and friends from the start. Some are stronger than others, some weaker, but with plenty of support most get through it somehow. I don't know anyone who isn't mentally scarred by the abuse they've suffered, but having plenty of moral support has helped some become survivors rather than victims. I never had any support, which is why I believe that it took me so long to realise that it does take time to heal. It also takes time to forgive and understand that they, the victims, themselves are in no way to blame.

I will never forgive my father, but I can say I understand that he has a serious problem. If he'd told the truth and faced up to his illness, I would have considered forgiving him, because I truly believe that anyone who would consider sexually abusing a child has got a serious mental illness. I know that there are some people out there who have had thoughts of that nature but go out and get the help that is required to stop it from turning into more than just a thought.

My father chose the other option of carrying his thoughts through into action. He truly believed in his mind that he was showing me the love of a father to a daughter. I know now that he believed that this was what fathers were supposed to do, because he'd seen that same love being shown to his sisters by his own father while he was growing up. I'm not giving him excuses. No, I believe that he had a choice, that he could have broken the cycle if he had truly wanted to. I know that he knew that he was wrong, otherwise he wouldn't still be lying now. Part of me feels sorry for him, because he'll never know what it is like to truly love your child, never wanting any harm to come to them, never having a sexual thought cross your mind, whenever you look at them. He will die a very lonely man, without his grandchildren and so unable to say to them, 'Look at what I've achieved in life.' He has achieved nothing more than the Devil could have done, and I believe that will haunt him for the rest of his life. Whether he shows that he is in pain because of what he's done to anyone around him is another matter. We can all hide behind a mask of lies, but deep down he knows the truth and his ghosts will follow him to the bitter end.

I managed to get rid of my ghosts while writing this book. It has truly helped me to get over some of the events that took over my life for a long time. If any of you have experienced anything in life that has caused you pain, I would suggest that you do the same.

Even nowadays, child abuse is such a taboo subject. So, if you have a story to tell and if you are truly ready to write about, go for it! There are too many stories like these left untold, and every story that is told leaves people shocked enough to take notice, stand up and try to stop the abuse. I won't say that writing the story of my life has been easy. It has been the most challenging, heartbreaking and life-changing thing that I've ever done. To bring back all those events to the forefront of my mind was very, very hard to do, but now it's out there I hope it will help people to see that this happens every day to your neighbours, friends, cousins, brothers and sisters and many of the people you see every day.

I feel that some good will come of my pain and suffering, so I don't mind the fact that I felt even more pain by putting pen to paper, because every story that is told could help yet another event unfold, which is my goal in life. I want child abuse stopped — right now! I know that I can't save the world, but it won't stop me from trying. Keep fighting! And be strong!

Sadly, Nana passed away two days after her 85th birthday and while I was trying to get my book published. I desperately tried to get my book out there for her before she died, yet it wasn't to be. But I know she was very proud of me, because she showed it every time I went to visit her by telling everyone in her nursing home at least five times an hour, 'She's written a book, you know. She's ever so clever. This is my granddaughter.'

It still hurts and feels very raw to me that she didn't get to see the finished product. I didn't even have a publisher at that time but I always promised her that I would get there, and so I'm pleased to have fulfilled my promise to Nana. I'm dedicating this book to her, and I can't thank her enough for the strength she gave me throughout my entire life. When I lost Nana, it felt as though it was the end of an era, and not only had I lost a friend, a lot of love and affection, but my real mother too. She knew that she didn't have to carry me for nine months for me to regard her as my mother, because she was the only person who behaved like a mother should. Fortunately, she has left me with the most wonderful memories, which I'm privileged to have from her. Watching and waiting for Nana to leave was a very traumatic experience for me. I sat with her every day, hoping and praying that she would have the strength to fight her illness and stay with me for a few more years. Sometimes I wished for extra days, hours, minutes, anything, rather than to have to let her go. I had mixed emotions about her dying and often felt selfish for trying everything in my power to keep her alive. And then when I saw her in pain I occasionally wished for her to die, so her suffering would be over. But when I missed the moment she died by minutes, after taking a break from being by her bedside for an hour, it hit me really hard, and, although I'd been saying goodbye to her for two weeks, as she lay on her deathbed, it wasn't enough. I wanted more. I wanted to say goodbye one more time.

So here's my way of saying goodbye, thousands of times. Nana was the only person, other than my children, who was constant in my life. For that, I will always love her. She is with Granddad now, and hopefully they are both very happy, wherever they are. This is for both of you.

Thank you for believing in me. I will never forget you.